RENAISSANCE

TIME
LIFE
BOOKS
®

LIFE WORLD LIBRARY

LIFE NATURE LIBRARY

TIME READING PROGRAM

THE LIFE HISTORY OF THE UNITED STATES

LIFE SCIENCE LIBRARY

GREAT AGES OF MAN

TIME-LIFE LIBRARY OF ART

TIME-LIFE LIBRARY OF AMERICA

FOODS OF THE WORLD

THIS FABULOUS CENTURY

LIFE LIBRARY OF PHOTOGRAPHY

GREAT AGES OF MAN

A History of the World's Cultures

RENAISSANCE

by

JOHN R. HALE

and

The Editors of TIME-LIFE BOOKS

TIME-LIFE BOOKS, NEW YORK

THE AUTHOR: John R. Hale is chairman of the Department of History at the University of Warwick in England. Formerly a Fellow and Tutor at Jesus College, Oxford, he has taught at Cornell University. He is widely regarded as one of Britain's leading Renaissance scholars. His publications include *England and the Italian Renaissance*, *Machiavelli and Renaissance Italy*, *The Evolution of British Historiography*, and a volume of translations of Machiavelli's letters and plays.

THE CONSULTING EDITOR: Leonard Krieger, Professor of History at Columbia University, was formerly Professor of History at Yale. Dr. Krieger is the author of *The German Idea of Freedom* and *The Politics of Discretion* and co-author of *History*, written in collaboration with John Higham and Felix Gilbert.

THE COVER: A chalk drawing depicts a mercenary captain, one of the many *condottieri* who served all of the Renaissance Italian states in their interminable wars.

TIME-LIFE BOOKS

EDITOR
Jerry Korn

EXECUTIVE EDITOR
A. B. C. Whipple

PLANNING
Oliver E. Allen

TEXT DIRECTOR   ART DIRECTOR
Martin Mann   Sheldon Cotler

CHIEF OF RESEARCH
Beatrice T. Dobie

PICTURE EDITOR
Robert G. Mason

Assistant Text Directors:
Ogden Tanner, Diana Hirsh
Assistant Art Director: Arnold C. Holeywell
Assistant Chief of Research: Martha T. Goolrick
Assistant Picture Editor: Melvin L. Scott

PUBLISHER
Joan D. Manley
General Manager: John D. McSweeney
Business Manager: John Steven Maxwell
Sales Director: Carl G. Jaeger
Promotion Director: Beatrice K. Tolleris
Public Relations Director: Nicholas Benton

GREAT AGES OF MAN

SERIES EDITOR: Russell Bourne
Editorial Staff for *Renaissance:*
Editor: Harold C. Field
Assistant Editors: Betsy Frankel, Carlotta Kerwin
Designer: Norman Snyder
Copy Editor: Paul Trachtman
Staff Writers: Gerald Simons, Edmund White
Picture Research: Dori Watson
Text Research: Terry Drucker,
Carol Isenberg, Irene Ertugrul,
Patricia Skinner, Linda Wolfe

EDITORIAL PRODUCTION
Production Editor: Douglas B. Graham
Quality Director: Robert L. Young
Assistant: James J. Cox
Copy Staff: Rosalind Stubenberg, Florence Keith
Picture Department: Dolores A. Littles, Patricia Maye
Traffic: Arthur A. Goldberger, David Wyland
Art Assistants: Anne Landry, Robert Pellegrini, Leonard Wolfe

The following individuals and departments of Time Inc. gave valuable aid in the preparation of this book: Editorial Production, Robert W. Boyd Jr.; Editorial Reference, Peter Draz; Picture Collection, Doris O'Neil; Photographic Laboratory, George Karas; TIME-LIFE News Service, Richard M. Clurman; Correspondents Ann Natanson, Erik Amfitheatrof (Rome), Katharine Sachs (London) and Maria Vincenza Aloisi (Paris).

CONTENTS

NOTE: THE PRESENT LOCATIONS OF ALL WORKS OF ART REPRODUCED IN THIS BOOK, AND THE NAMES OF THEIR CREATORS, ARE LISTED ON PAGES 186-187.

INTRODUCTION

Nowadays historians habitually break history into ages or periods—the Homeric Age; the Periclean Age; the Middle Ages; the Renaissance; the Enlightenment; and others. Among all these ages the Renaissance in Italy holds a special place. First, it is the subject of the most famous of histories of a civilization, Jacob Burckhardt's *The Civilization of the Renaissance in Italy*, written a century ago. Because Burckhardt's book has been so long preeminent and because it focused on Italy in the 15th Century, it made the history of that place and time the forum in which the general problems of the history of civilization were earliest discussed and have been most vigorously dealt with. Thus for a long while the Renaissance was, and perhaps it still remains, the best laboratory for the study of a historical period.

Moreover, the Renaissance era in Italy is the first age in the history of civilization *to discover itself* as an age. The Egyptians of the Old Kingdom, the Middle Kingdom and the New Empire, and the Europeans of the Middle Ages did not think of themselves as living in those particular epochs. But many of the leading men of the age of the Renaissance were acutely conscious of living in a new era of human history, an era marked primarily not by its political organization or its religion, but by its civilization.

In *Renaissance*, Professor John Hale has performed a remarkable and admirable threefold feat of history writing. In the first place he has captured and transmitted the sense of excitement with which Italians of the Renaissance greeted their two great discoveries—their discovery of classical antiquity and their correlative discovery of themselves. These two produced a burst of achievement in scholarship, literature and especially in architecture, sculpture and painting, that has ever since remained a wonder of the world. As his story gradually comes to a brilliant focus on the living center of the Renaissance, the city of Florence in the 15th Century, Professor Hale dispels the miasma of myth that for some has concealed rather than disclosed the age of the Renaissance—a spurious compound of frivolity, swagger, unrestrained violence, uninhibited lechery and unlimited assassination. The creators of Renaissance Florence were sober men, mostly businessmen, family men, and in an unspectacular way religious men; and they built a soberly beautiful city whose great monuments are its magnificent religious buildings and its great private houses and the paintings and sculptures with which its citizens adorned them.

Secondly, having engaged his readers with the spirit of the Renaissance, Professor Hale stands back from the spectacle and seeks the peculiar conjuncture of circumstances that fostered that extraordinary flowering of genius, 500 years ago, which had as its center a city a good bit smaller than Trenton, New Jersey. Employing the best and newest historical investigations, he relates the geography of Italy, the economic and social characteristics of the life of its cities, its eccentric political development, and the intellectual labors of its scholars to the achievements of the Renaissance.

Finally he adapts his prose style to his purpose; for he writes like what he writes about. His style is clear, vigorous and sober, yet illuminated with flashes of wit and sharpened by shrewd, hard-headed observations. In this he writes in a way that harmonizes elegantly with the way the Florentines, who above all made the Renaissance, lived.

J. H. HEXTER
Yale University

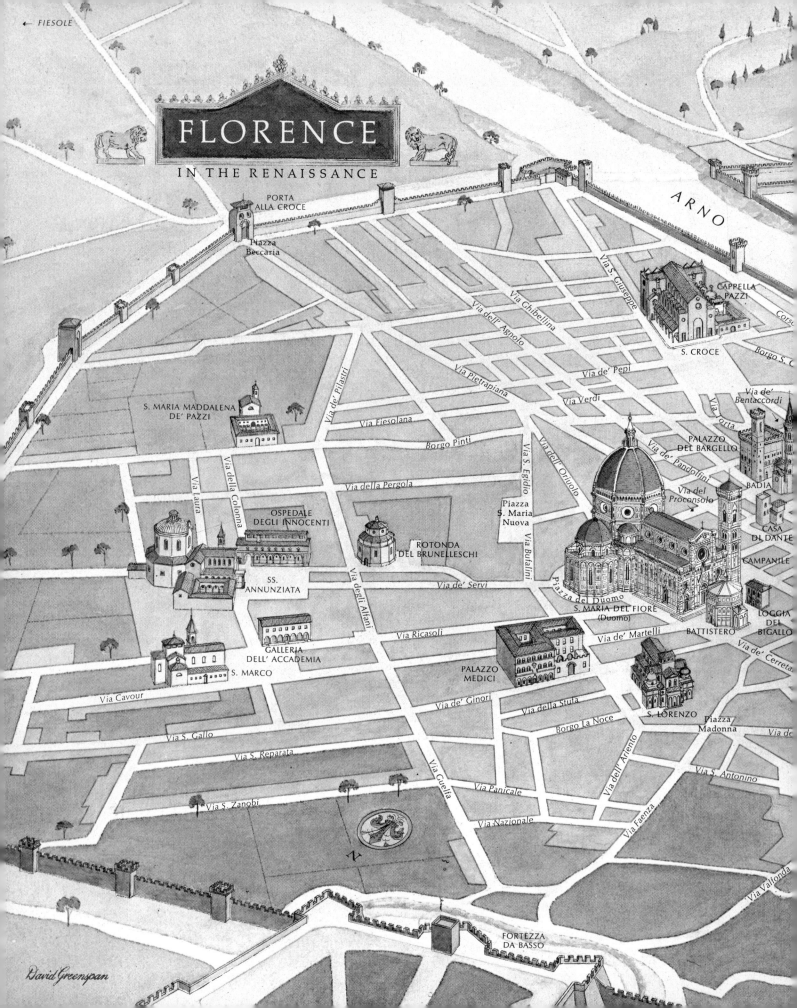

PORTA
S. NICCOLO

S. MINIATO
AL MONTE

Via dell' Erta Canina

FORTEZZA
DI BELVEDERE

Via di Belvedere

Via di S. Leonardo

Via di S. Niccolo

Lungarno Serristori

Lungarno delle Grazie

Via' Tintori

Via de' Benci

PONTE
ALLE GRAZIE

Lungarno Torrigiani

Via de' Bardi

Costa a S. Giorgio

GIARDINO
DI BOBOLI

PALAZZO
VECCHIO

Via
de' Saponai

GALLERIA
DEGLI UFFIZI

S. FELICITA

PALAZZO
GONDI

Piazza
della Signoria

LOGGIA DEL LANZI

PALAZZO PITTI

OR
S. MICHELE

Via Por S. Maria

PALAZZO
DAVANZATI

PONTE
VECCHIO

S. IACOPO
OLTRARNO

Via de' Guicciardini

Calimala

LOGGIA
DI MERCATO NUOVO

PALAZZO
SPINI

Via dei Speziali

Via Pellicceria

Via delle Terme

Via Maggio

a Brunelleschi

Via Porta Rossa

S. SPIRITO

Via de' Vecchietti

PONTE
S. TRINITA

Lungarno Corsini

Lungarno Guicciardini

Via de' Pescioni

PALAZZO
STROZZI

Via de' Tornabuoni

S. TRINITA

Via del Parione

Via de' Serragli

Via delle Belle Donne

PALAZZO RUCELLAI

Piazza
Goldoni

PONTE
ALLA CARRAIA

S. MARIA
DEL CARMINE

iglio

Via de' Panzani

Via del Moro

Via de' Fossi

Borgo S. Frediano

S. MARIA
NOVELLA

Via del Porcellana

OGNISSANTI

Via della Scala

Via Palazzuolo

Borgo Ognissanti

Via Montebello

PORTA
S. FREDIANO

Via degli Orti Oricellari

1

THE BREAK
WITH THE MIDDLE AGES

ENRAPTURED SINGERS, *in a 15th Century relief, were carved for a choir loft of Florence's cathedral. "People run into the churches as if they were theaters," Erasmus observed, "for the sake of the sensuous charm of the ear."*

Human nature does not change much. Men have always liked food and warmth, raised families, felt happier when the sun shone than when it rained, wanted peace and fought wars, created delicate works of art and committed violent crimes. Yet there have been periods in history when men thought that the lives they lived and the ideas they held made their age strikingly different from the one before it. Of all such ages the Italian Renaissance is perhaps the most famous. The men of the Renaissance thought of their time as one in which mankind changed fundamentally.

Later historians have sometimes agreed, sometimes disagreed with this point of view. Did the Italian Renaissance represent a complete break with the Middle Ages? Did it see the birth of Modern Man? Would a 20th Century man feel at home if a time machine could transport him back to Venice or Florence or Rome in the age of Petrarch, Machiavelli and Leonardo da Vinci? How different was Renaissance man from his medieval predecessors? How different was he from the man of today?

The important development that we call the Renaissance actually began in Italy in the waning years of the Middle Ages, about 1300 A.D. Giotto, the most revolutionary painter of his day, was then 33; Dante, author of the *Divine Comedy*, 35. By the middle of the 14th Century, the Renaissance had become a distinct and recognizable cultural movement. Over the course of the next 200 years—until the sack of Rome by the soldiers of Charles V, ruler of the Germanic empire beyond the Alps—the world as Dante and Giotto saw it was transformed. Men and nature were treated not as generalizations of themselves, but as individual beings and things, interesting for their own sake.

In a typical painting of the late 13th Century the human figures are flat and unreal—it is difficult to imagine them speaking. Buildings are symbolic objects, not places to live in; the landscape is decorative but impossible to walk through. Near things and far, big things and small are shown without relation to each other; everything is confused. The artist indicates trees and hills, but he does not open a window onto a particular, believable piece of the world.

By the 15th Century, however, painters were

ITALY DURING THE RENAISSANCE

A PATCHWORK OF STATES, *studded with important cities, is revealed in this map of Renaissance Italy. The various state boundaries (broken lines) became relatively stable in 1454, when the Peace of Lodi ended a long period of internecine wars. In 1455 the five chief powers—Milan, Venice, Florence, Naples and the* Papal States—*formed the Italian League, primarily to prevent any member from gaining dominance. A shaky political balance was maintained until the French invasions began in 1494. During this 40-year period of general peace, the city-states were bustling centers of art and culture, and the Renaissance neared its apogee.*

painting animated, three-dimensional people; it is possible to look at Ghirlandaio's men and women and imagine what they are thinking or are about to say. The rooms they walk through and the countryside beyond are a record of what these things really look like: the artist is looking at the world with something like a photographer's eye. But how far does this record of reality—as presented by the poets and statesmen of the period, as well as the artists—correspond with modern notions of reality? Were the men of the Renaissance truly as different from medieval men as they seem? Or is the difference simply one of changing fashions in the way men wrote and painted and sculpted?

There is no doubt about the opinion of the people of the time. It was Renaissance Italians who invented the term "Dark Ages." They looked back on the barbarian invasion of Rome as the drawing down of a coarse blind, and on the intervening 10 centuries as a period of trance. It was, to them, both a joy and a duty to force the blind up again, to breathe life into the literature, the monuments and the values that had made Rome great.

To this task they brought a growing spirit of confidence, strengthened by the existence of men of genius in every branch of art and learning. There were poets and scholars like Petrarch and Boccaccio, sculptors like Donatello, architects like Brunelleschi, painters like Masaccio—to pick out only a few. No wonder Matteo Palmieri, writing in the mid-15th Century, could joyfully exhort his fellow man to "thank God that it has been permitted to him to be born in this new age, so full of hope and promise, which already rejoices in a greater array of nobly-gifted souls than the world has seen in the thousand years that have preceded it." No wonder the Renaissance architect Antonio Filarete could characterize the Middle Ages as a crude era, one in which "learning was lacking in Italy, people became vulgar in speech and ignorant

of Latin," and observe that it was only 50 or 60 years before his own time "that men's minds were sharpened and awakened."

The learning that Filarete was referring to was a secular learning. In contrast to the largely theological studies of the Middle Ages, it was based on an avid study of classical authors. To go forward it was necessary to go back; to advance from the Middle Ages it was necessary to return to antiquity and relearn the lessons which had enabled Rome to produce her great civilization. Medieval scholars had known about men like Vergil, Ovid and Cicero, Aristotle and Plato; but not until the 14th Century, and then only in Italy, was an attempt made to see the whole classical world as a culture in its own right. The study of this culture came to be called humanism. And humanists were concerned not only with discovering and editing Greek and Roman books, but with sorting out those elements in ancient thought which could help men live better, more responsible lives. They turned to Rome not only for instruction about law, politics and the arts, but even for moral guidance.

The key to understanding this fascination with antiquity lies in the economic and political life of the Italian states—"Italian states" rather than "Italy" because the dissolution of the Roman Empire had also dissolved the peninsula's political unity. Northern Italy became part of the old Empire's young successor, the German-centered, German-governed Holy Roman Empire. Central Italy was dominated by the political power of the papacy. A branch of the French dynastic house of Anjou ruled southern Italy as the Kingdom of Naples. But even these divisions were not cohesive within themselves. In the north, the city-states of Venice and Milan went their own way, independent of the Germanic emperors. In the center, important towns like Bologna were largely free from papal influence. And from the late 13th Century onward there was constant rivalry between the Kingdom of Naples and various Sicilian cities and towns controlled by the Spanish house of Aragon.

Until the beginning of the 14th Century, none of these individual political units was sufficiently autonomous or prosperous to produce a vigorous culture of its own. Then, in the comparatively brief period of a few decades, autonomy was achieved in a series of crises.

In 1305 the papacy left Rome, finding that brawls among the major Roman families made its continued existence there intolerable. It went north into France and settled, finally, at Avignon, where it stayed for 70 years. In its absence the former papal territories were divided among leading local families and became independent city-states. Shortly afterward, in 1313, northern Italy also gained independence. Henry VII, ruler of the Holy Roman Empire, lost political control of the province of Lombardy, leaving the northern Italian cities free to pursue their own interests without glancing constantly across the Alps for approval. At the same time, Robert of Anjou, King of Naples, attempted and failed to dominate all of Italy, and in the process weakened his hold over his own southern territories. Although never entirely free from the threat of outside influence (France, Spain and Germany all continued to have ambitions on the peninsula), the cities and states of Italy were at last in a position to think almost exclusively about themselves.

By this time the larger Italian cities were thrivingly prosperous. Italy as a whole had the immense advantage of being situated right in the heart of the greatest trading area in the medieval and Renaissance world, the Mediterranean basin. Coastal towns like Genoa and Venice had unique opportunities, and took them. In addition, many of the goods imported by sea were redistributed by land, bringing prosperity to towns like Florence, whose location made it a hub for such traffic, or like Milan, which became a way station for transalpine export into the heart of Europe.

This precocious economic development produced a power structure that was peculiarly Italian. Instead of being centered in the great landed estate, as elsewhere in Europe, power was centered in the town. Beginning in the 12th Century, the feudal lords of the Italian countryside had been forced to become citizens of the nearest town. Only by doing so could they share in its prosperity and retain some semblance of political influence over its government. By the late 13th Century this urbanization of power was complete. Florence had risen to such an impressive combination of wealth and social coherence that it could challenge a Pope. When Boniface VIII demanded that the Florentine government reverse a sentence that displeased him, Florence replied that he had no business interfering in "the policies and decisions of the Florentine commune."

By the 14th Century, through the accumulating profits of trade and industry, Italian cities had become lavish patrons of the arts. Florence, for example, had begun to build its vast cathedral, Santa Maria del Fiore. Not even a period of depression, aggravated by the Black Death—the terrible plague that devastated Europe in the middle of the 14th Century—failed to stem the flow of patronage. When profits fell, Italian merchants and bankers learned to become more efficient in their business methods. It was Italians who pioneered much of what later became standard capitalist practice: partnership agreements, holding companies, marine insurance, credit transfers, double-entry bookkeeping. And, as the depression deepened, Italian businessmen invested in culture for its permanence of value, much as anxious businessmen buy fashionable art today.

Wealth, however, cannot buy culture, it can only

DISPUTING WITH THE DOCTORS *in the temple at Jerusalem, a youthful Christ is pictured at the center of this glazed Renaissance plate. The border of the plate, densely decorated with a variety of musical instruments, tradesmen's tools and implements of war, reflects the spirit of an age that did not separate religious and secular interests.*

buy its works. Culture is nourished by money, but its nucleus is a wider exposure to learning. During the Renaissance, to get rich and to stay rich required a relatively high standard of education. First and foremost, this education was utilitarian: a man could not be successful in commerce and industry without knowing how to read and write and being skillful at figures. But the ways of the Renaissance world required something further. More business meant more partnership agreements, more complicated wills, more conveyancing—in short, more law. Legal studies boomed steadily throughout the Renaissance, attracting the largest enrollment at universities, and causing professors of law to be paid among the highest of academic salaries. And as the city-states grew, the business of government became more complicated, creating a demand for a well-educated secretariat at home and for diplomats who could speak with persuasion and eloquence abroad.

There was, then, a steadily increasing pressure for a more practical kind of education than the one provided by the theological studies of the Middle Ages. Professional skills were needed—also worldly attitudes. The humanistic program of studies took shape to provide them. This program involved the reading of ancient authors and the study of such subjects as grammar, rhetoric, history and moral philosophy. By the 15th Century such a course was officially known as *studia humanitatis*, or "humanities," and the men who pursued this knowledge came to be known as humanists.

Humanism means something different today, but in the Renaissance it stood for a view of life that, while devoutly accepting the existence of God, shared many of the intellectual attitudes of the ancient pagan world. It was interested in esthetics, saw the usefulness of a knowledge of history, and was convinced that man's chief duty was to enjoy his life soberly and serve his community actively. Thus

15

humanism restored to balance the scales which the Middle Ages had tilted with a concern for eternity. It stressed earthly fulfillment rather than preparation for paradise. It had its spiritual side, but it reflected a society that was more interested in worldly matters—a society that was practical, canny, self-conscious and ambitious.

But humanism could not become a real movement, involving a whole society, until that society had a positive need to learn about the classical past —until it saw in the wisdom of Rome an answer to its own problems. The classical revival was preceded not only by modifications in the small world of medieval university curricula, but by an irrational yearning for change that spread through the whole medieval world. The Middle Ages may look static, but in fact they were characterized by considerable dissatisfaction. Men sensed that things were not going as they should—in either church or state—and longed for some sort of regeneration, some sort of revival. Rome, once the secular as well as the spiritual capital of the world, became the focus of these aspirations. Men yearned for the rebirth, the renaissance, of Rome's past glories.

Paradoxically, the first activists in this movement arose within a profession that normally opposes change: the law. To meet the demands of a more complex society and a more involved economy, lawyers began to re-examine the great codes of ancient Roman law, the *Digest* and the *Codex*. Instead of simply relying on abstracts prepared by medieval commentators, they began to pay attention to what had been in the minds of the actual compilers of these great legacies. And in the course of relating their problems to decisions handed down in antiquity, they had to imagine the conditions of life in ancient Rome. This led them to other classical works and, inevitably, from reading for business to reading for pleasure. Thus a highly conservative profession became a hotbed of pioneers intent upon carrying out humanist reform.

By the end of the 13th Century, lawyers in the northern Italian cities, especially in Padua and Verona, were displaying a lively interest in the poetry, as well as the history and law, of ancient Rome. They were searching in libraries for forgotten manuscripts and reading them with scholarly zest. Like their humanist successors, they were concerned with establishing the correct words of a text and attributing them to the right author. This desire to rub the patina from medieval glosses, and bring up the original, bright and clear, gave the Renaissance a firsthand knowledge of what the ancients had actually said, and enabled it to speak with them directly, across the centuries.

It is difficult to imagine the excitement that attended this unearthing of new and purer texts, this tuning in on voices that spoke with such joy and conviction about the noblest, most triumphant age that Italy has ever known. Above all, since most of the ancient writers studied were Roman, it was an intensely personal excitement. The Italian humanists were discovering their own ancestors, finding buried treasure in their own house. To Petrarch, Cicero was not just a dusty sage, but a real person to whom he could write a letter—and did. To Machiavelli, banished from political life, living in squalor and inactivity on a small farm outside Florence, nothing was sweeter than to lock himself away in his study; there he could forget the humiliating present and "converse" with the great Roman figures of the past, learning how they coped with the crises of their world, applying their solutions to the crises of his own.

This desire to imitate and learn from the long-dead Romans led men of the Renaissance to study principally the historians, men like Livy and Tacitus. But the writings of such men as Quintilian and Cicero were almost as important. Their theories on education, on the qualities of character and mind that best suited a man to meet the challenges of the Roman world, were thought to be equally applicable to the world of the 14th and 15th Centuries. One Roman quality particularly stressed was that of all-round competence, which became the hallmark of Renaissance man. It was from these Roman theorists also that the Renaissance adopted the belief that a man's learning should be put at the disposal of others, that he should live an active civic life rather than revel privately in the delights of scholarship.

Consequently, while many medieval scholars had been recluses, concerned with solitary meditations on metaphysical matters, the Renaissance scholar was much more likely to be a public figure—a teacher, a propagandist, a diplomat, a secretary of state. Even a Pope could subscribe to this view. In his treatise on education, written in the middle of the 15th Century, Aeneas Silvius Piccolomini, then a bishop but later to become Pius II, deprecated an overabsorption in studies like dialectic and geometry because they diverted a boy's attention from real life. Teachers turned their backs on the medieval idealization of poverty, celibacy and seclusion, and instead praised family life and the wise use of riches. A monastery cell and unwashed feet were no longer felt to be prerequisites for the development of the mind; learning was best pursued in some degree of material comfort. Man's role in history was no longer a passive one in which he waited fatalistically for death or the Second Coming of Christ. Physical adversity was regarded not as the inevitable punishment for sin but as the aimless working of chance, a whim of the goddess Fortuna. And Fortuna could be countered by sharp-eyed resourcefulness.

In fact, Fortuna was one of the two most popular emblems of the Renaissance; the other was Occasio, opportunity. Fortuna is often shown in a boat, with a rudder and sail so that a man can direct her. But sometimes she merges with Occasio to become a hurrying woman, long hair waving forward from the front of her head, entirely bald in the back. All was well if a man moved swiftly enough to seize her forelock; all was lost if he grabbed too late. Chance was no longer something to dread, but something to take advantage of. Prudence and skill—active qualities that allowed a man to manipulate his destiny—became more popular than wise saws that put man's fate in the hands of God. The dolphin-and-anchor emblem of the famous Renaissance publishing house, the Aldine press, summed up the ideal of the age: activity tempered by restraint—the dolphin's speed, the anchor's drag.

Although it is true that Renaissance Italy was publicly violent and given to grandiloquent displays, the most singular element in the private life of the times may have been moderation. Men were able to accept opposing points of view. They did not challenge Christian doctrine, but neither did they think it the only source of guidance for an honorable and useful life. Thinkers like Pico della Mirandola drew upon Plato, upon the religious teaching of Persia, upon Arabic philosophy, upon the Jewish cabala. Writers like Petrarch and Leon Battista Alberti saw no conflict between the moral teaching of Cicero and the Christian ethic. While medieval theology was still taken for granted, men turned their attention to elaborating a philosophy of man.

In the Middle Ages to praise man was to praise God, for man was a creation of God. But Renaissance writers praised man himself as a creator. They played down the sinfulness he was born with and emphasized his ability to think and act for himself, to produce works of art, to guide the destiny of others. They freed man from his pegged place in the medieval hierarchy, halfway between matter and spirit, and allowed him to roam at will, through all the levels of being, sometimes identifying himself with the brutes, sometimes with the angels. He was seen as the ruler of nature—the lord, although not the Lord, of creation.

This new vision of man sprang from a heightened awareness of self. Medieval men had been preoccupied with searching their souls, but Renaissance men were much more intrigued with exploring, and indeed parading, their own personalities. Petrarch is a perfect example. Although his serious interests centered on his work in discovering and editing ancient texts, Petrarch was also interested in himself. In his letters, designed for posterity as well as his friends, he left a record of his reactions to love affairs and friendship, to mountains and the flowers in his garden. They are an intellectual and emotional self-portrait, the first since antiquity.

It was in this same spirit of self-interest that men began to call attention to themselves as unique and individual beings. Composers began to sign their music. Around 1340 a self-confident Florentine banker had the audacity to have his portrait painted for his tomb, and in 1453 Piero de' Medici commissioned a portrait bust of himself. One of Michelangelo's greatest sculptures, the Julius monument for St. Peter's in Rome, celebrated a single Pope—on the Pope's orders. Another of Michelangelo's designs, the chapel for the Church of San Lorenzo in Florence, was commissioned by the Medici to memorialize two members of their family. And an interest in one man as an individual prompted Boccaccio, in his life of Dante, to attempt to describe a man's personality instead of merely rattling off a string of edifying anecdotes about his accomplishments.

But humanism was not an unmixed blessing. While the rediscovery of the culture of ancient Rome speeded Renaissance man in the direction he wanted to go, it also imposed its own itinerary. In some ways it was not a good one. Take, for example, language. A man can best explain himself and his world in his own language, the vernacular. Dante, Petrarch and Boccaccio were all intensely and successfully personal writers in the common tongue of their day—but they were prestigious exceptions. Almost everyone else was influenced by Rome; it became fashionable to write in Latin. Not until late in the 15th Century, when the powerful Lorenzo de' Medici chose to compose poems in the dialect of the Tuscan common man, did the vernacular begin to gain respectability. Then, through the works of men like Machiavelli and Castiglione, literature assumed its primary function of helping a society to understand itself.

The influence of the past was strengthened by the fact that the Renaissance had no conception of evolutionary progress. Men did not believe, as modern men do (with misgivings), that society can steadily improve itself by inventing new ways to exploit natural resources and organize economies and governments. Their impulse was to rediscover, not invent. They sought to improve man's condition not by looking forward to the frontiers of knowledge, but by looking back to its reservoirs. It seemed to the Renaissance that the ancients had done nearly everything about as well as it could be done. Change was possible; indeed, each new generation of painters was praised because it was "more modern" than the last. But "more modern," to the Renaissance, really meant closer to the precepts laid down by Rome.

It is never altogether healthy for a society to model itself on the past—men's attitudes and the circumstances of their lives change too much. To "think like a Roman" was helpful in some spheres, like politics or law; irrelevant in others, like business; disruptive in still others, like religion. If the Renaissance had its dark side, its pessimism and discontent, some of the uneasiness was surely due to this fact. Renaissance intellectuals were trying

INNOVATION IN PORTRAITURE, *Mino da Fiesole's realistic study of Piero de' Medici, done in 1453, was the first portrait bust made since the fall of ancient Rome. Piero's composure is all the more remarkable because chronic illness plagued him throughout his life. The Florentines called him "il Gottoso," or "the Gouty." According to Machiavelli, he was often so wracked that "he could use no faculty but that of speech."*

to travel in shoes that had been borrowed from other men, and the shoes did not always fit.

But there was another source of this discontent. This was the demand made upon the individual by the new attitude toward knowledge. In the Middle Ages the painter, the philosopher, the writer had used their talents for a single purpose—to praise God and make His purposes plain. But in the Renaissance each branch of intellectual activity became distinct from other branches, and each was justified in terms of its means rather than its end. That is, a painting succeeded in terms of its excellence as a painting, quite apart from the purpose for which it was painted.

For art and science to evolve, this disassociation from a common purpose was essential. A painter must study art for art's sake before painting can advance technically. A politician must study the science of governing to deal effectively with political crises. But as the branches of the tree of knowledge grow outward, the shade beneath it ceases to be so snug and sheltering. When a painter becomes conscious of technique, a certain harmony between him and his object is destroyed. When a politician has to choose between morality and expediency, it places a burden on his conscience. Renaissance men struggled with these problems, and the pain they experienced in the struggle is familiar. In our day, too, knowledge has outstripped our ability to come to terms with it. But would the problems themselves seem familiar to us? Some would, and some would not.

Certainly we would recognize the general concern for political and constitutional issues. Although the Renaissance had no mass media to keep public opinion informed, the smallness of the Italian states made it possible for their citizens to know what was going on. And the ephemeral nature of most of the governments produced a steady stream of domestic crises and scandals to whet public interest. Furthermore, until the 16th Century, when foreign monarchs dominated some parts of Italy and princely dynasties ruled others, power was in theory in the hands of the people.

We would also recognize the attitudes of the Renaissance businessman and lawyer, and the feeling of the Renaissance artist that he was a genius, not just a craftsman. We could echo—with perhaps a few reservations—the confident assertion made by Gianozzo Manetti in 1452 that God may have created the world but that thereafter man transformed and improved it: "For everything that surrounds us is our own work, the work of man: all dwellings, all castles, all cities, all the edifices throughout the whole world, which are so numerous and of such quality that they resemble the works of angels rather than men. Ours are the paintings, the sculptures; ours are the trades, sciences and philosophical systems. Ours are all inventions and all kinds of languages and literary works, and when we think about their necessary employment, we are compelled so much the more to admiration and astonishment."

Finally we would recognize the intellectual concerns of the Renaissance scholar, his search for truth and his willingness to attack long-held beliefs when they seemed false. The activities of Lorenzo Valla, for instance, would not seem strange to us. In 1440 Valla wrote a treatise proving that the *Donation of Constantine* was a forgery. Since the *Donation*, a document allegedly written in the Fourth Century, formed the basis of the papacy's claim to territorial power in Italy, Valla's attack was shocking. But his methods were those that scholars still use today: through critical study of word usage and historical references, he showed that the document could not have been written until the Eighth Century. And his philosophical position was stated in terms that might have been used by a modern intellectual: "To give one's life in defense of truth

and justice is the path of the highest virtue, the highest honor, the highest reward."

But there is one element in Renaissance intellectual life that would seem strange to us: despite outward appearances, its scientific outlook had almost nothing in common with our own. Leonardo da Vinci could say, "It seems to me that those sciences are vain and full of error which do not spring from experiment, the source of all certainty," but Leonardo was talking about the construction of locks and canals and the building of machines, not investigations of the physical universe for the discovery of general laws.

For a knowledge of such matters the Renaissance, once again, went back to the classics—to Aristotle for physics, to Galen for medicine. Scientific curiosity was mostly devoted to fact-finding, and the inspiration for this was provided not by science itself, but by art. It was art that pioneered the study of anatomy and the construction of systems of mathematical perspective. The experiments the Renaissance conducted were, by and large, experiments to find out how a thing worked. And the purpose of the experiment often seems trivial: Leonardo's famed "flying machine" was designed to make a chariot-drawn model of an angel flap its wings as it was pulled through the streets of Milan during one of the city's numerous carnivals.

The revolution in ideas about the physical nature of man and the universe did not get under way until the Renaissance was nearly over—not until 1543 did Copernicus publish his work on the solar system and Vesalius, in the same year, publish his work on human anatomy. But the Renaissance collected a good part of the material that sparked the revolution and, more important, it initiated the intellectual attitudes that made the revolution possible. Renaissance man may not have been the "first modern man," but he was surely his immediate precursor.

AN AVID ANTIQUARIAN, *the rich Venetian Andrea Odoni admires his famous collection of ancient art in this portrait by Lorenzo Lotto.*

A PASSION FOR THE PAST

In mid-14th Century Italy, humanism was an idea whose hour had come. Its appeal—to revive and share in the glories of classical antiquity—proved irresistible to an urbane elite jaded with the faith-oriented culture of the Middle Ages. Men of learning, genius and wealth embraced the new movement with missionary zeal. They eulogized Latin as "the sweetest, richest and most cultured" of all languages. Latin literature and Greek ideals became the basis of an elaborate program of classical education. With boundless energy humanists excavated ruins, created libraries and filled their homes with a splendid bric-a-brac of ancient coins, vases and statuary. Just as their cause gave the age its name (Renaissance means "rebirth"), their zest and self-confidence set the temper of the time.

FOUNTAINHEAD OF
A NEW AGE

In seeking knowledge and inspiration, the Italian humanists turned first to their cultural fountainhead, the city of Rome. One of their greatest scholars, Poggio Bracciolini, spoke for them all when, viewing the results of centuries of callous neglect, he lamented that the ancient capital "now lies prostrate like a giant corpse, decayed and everywhere eaten away." The noble Forum, seen at right in a painting by the Flemish sojourner Paul Brill, had become a slum for squatters (*left*) and a pasture for livestock (*right*). It was popularly called the "*Campo Vaccino*," or the "*Cowfield*."

From the ruined city the humanists wrung a bountiful harvest. In the 1440s the papal secretary Flavio Biondo, who has been called the father of modern archeology, systematically catalogued the surviving monuments. In his two encyclopedic works, *Rome Triumphant* and *Rome Restored*, he used relics, inscriptions and early chronicles to give the Renaissance its first real look at the manners and customs, the forums and arenas of imperial Rome. Thereafter excavators working under a succession of antiquarian popes made many momentous finds, unearthing such celebrated works of ancient sculpture as the *Apollo Belvedere*, the *Vatican Venus* and, amid the rubble of the Baths of Titus, the powerful *Laocoön*.

By the early 1500s a century of excavation had transformed Rome into a vast museum. In 1519 Pope Leo X solemnized the humanists' wedding of the present and past by appointing the painter Raphael, one of the finest artists of the Renaissance, as superintendent of Rome's antiquities.

A DUTIFUL SCHOOLBOY *studies Cicero as a guide to a successful life. Many elite youths had humanist tutors; others—including some who were poor but gifted—attended schools run by humanists.*

SPREADING A NEW GOSPEL

The humanist credo enjoined its followers to transmit as well as to accumulate knowledge. Honoring this ideal, the classicists developed a rich curriculum and a cadre of dedicated educators. Clerics and noblemen spent fortunes to find and copy great works and to make them available to the public. The Duke of Urbino, creating what an aide called "the finest library since ancient times," kept 40 scribes busy for 14 years. One monk went into debt collecting classics; after his election as Pope Nicholas V, he acquired several thousand volumes which became the foundation of the Vatican library. Nicholas claimed no greater distinction than that he was generous "in the purchase of books, in the constant transcription of Greek and Latin manuscripts and in the rewarding of learned men."

A MODEL HUMANIST, *Cardinal Bessarion studies classical literature in a*

painting by Carpaccio. Equally devoted to scholarship and public service, the prelate gathered and donated 600 volumes to the city of Venice.

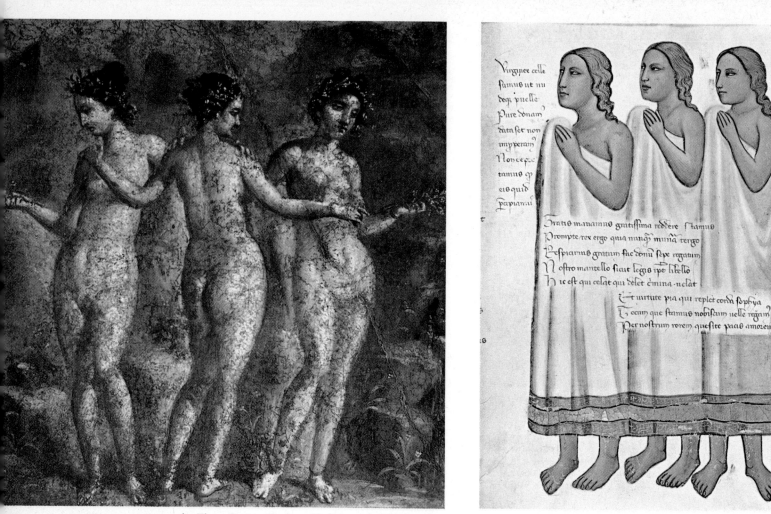

ANCIENT HANDMAIDENS, *the Three Graces—Verdure, Gladness and Splendor—do a sinuous dance in a robust Greco-Roman fresco painted in the First Century A.D.*

MEDIEVAL FIGURES *in a Tuscan manuscript, the Graces retreat behind a blanket inscribed with verses in Latin.*

AN ART IN PRAISE OF HUMAN BEAUTY

Humanism's debt to the classical past, and its rejection of medieval culture, are clearly revealed in the three works of art shown on these pages. All depict the Three Graces, attendants of the goddess of love. In the classical version, above at left, the Graces are full-bodied dancers, painted to idealize human beauty. In the Middle Ages, however, the human form was no longer admired for its own sake, and the Graces, above at right, became flat and bodiless. Humanists denounced such works as "A caricature of . . . human delineation."

The 15th Century painter Sandro Botticelli was no doctrinaire humanist, but his art radiates the spirit of the classical revival. His famous version of the Three Graces *(opposite)* restores them to joyful movement and once again revels in their beauty. To the ancient theme, Botticelli added the elegance, grace and new sophistication of his age.

RENAISSANCE GRACES, *a detail from Botticelli's "Primavera," display a rhythm and vitality stressed by their swirling veils.*

"THE SCHOOL OF ATHENS," *a fresco by Raphael, sums up classical knowledge and glorifies its Renaissance devotees by depicting great men from both*

ages in the same scene. At center Aristotle debates with a white-bearded Plato—whom Raphael portrayed with the features of Leonardo da Vinci.

2
THE VARIETY OF ITALY

THE MARBLE BAPTISTERY of *Pisa, a Romanesque and Gothic structure, was completed in the 14th Century. It stands in striking contrast to the medieval city walls in the distance and the baroque fountain in the foreground.*

Much of the vitality of the arts and political institutions of Renaissance Italy arose from the peninsula's physical diversity. At first glance it may seem as if Italy—surrounded on three sides by the sea, and guarded in the north by the towering arc of the Alps—ought to have something of the unity of an island. Instead, it is a land of fragments. It is divided, first of all, by its sheer length. Starting near the Teutonic heart of Europe, it runs some 700 miles south, to end only 100 miles from the Moslem coast of North Africa. It is also divided by the tilt of its axis, northwest to southeast, making Provence its neighbor at one pole and taking it to within 50 miles of Albania at the other. Finally, it is divided by the Apennines, the mountains that run like an arthritic backbone from Liguria in the northwest to Calabria in the south. Invading peoples washing down from the north and in from the sea drained away into scattered pools among the mountains' spurs.

Not surprisingly the early Italians turned their backs on the hostile and unprofitable mountains and looked outward, absorbing influences from abroad that made them still more unlike one another. The sea, which washed the varied flotsam of Mediterranean culture—Spanish, Arab, Greek—onto the peninsula's long coastline, also took Italian traders outward, to set up colonies in England, Spain and on the shores of the Black Sea. The Alpine passes, which had brought wave after wave of invasion into Italy, also carried Italian merchants north to the markets of Germany, France and the Low Countries. From all these places they brought back alien cultural influences. Milan, near the terminus of an Alpine pass to the north, has a German Gothic cathedral; Venice's splendid San Marco, many-domed, sheathed in marble and lined with mosaic, is like the Byzantine churches of Istanbul.

Geography and trade made Italians more cosmopolitan than homogeneous, and singularly local in their political outlook. Not until the 15th Century, responding to the innovations of Florentine art, did the rest of Italy look inward for an indigenous style in which to paint and carve and build. Not until the second half of the 19th Century did all Italians rally round a common flag.

The history of Renaissance Italy has then to be written in parallel columns—one for the monarchy of Naples, one each for the republics of Florence and Venice, one for the dukedom of Milan, one each for the petty despots who controlled—or tried to control—the political fates of cities like Rimini, Faenza, Imola, Forlì. To understand the Renaissance it is not necessary to follow the fate of all of them, but it is essential to grasp this fact: that Italy, in its variety, offered unique opportunities in art and politics and business.

Geography, of course, was not the only factor that prevented political union. Ever since the Middle Ages Italy had been divided in its loyalties between Guelph and Ghibelline—between the forces that supported the authority of the papacy and those that supported the authority of the secular rulers of the Holy Roman Empire. Cities, and factions within cities, supported first one side and then the other, depending upon which offered greater advantages. This pattern of shifting loyalties persisted even when the original rivalry ceased—as it did by the end of the 13th Century—to have any real force. It persisted in a system of flexible alliances, a sort of rudimentary balance-of-power arrangement, that prevented any one city from accumulating too much authority.

Not that any state ever really thought of controlling the whole of Italy: the Renaissance had no conception of the larger political unit called a nation. Although city-states constantly tried to expand, pushing and rubbing against one another's borders in a constant friction of small wars, the reasons were always limited and local—prestige, greed, security. Ultimately the most successful cities became territorial states, but none possessed the bureaucratic equipment, the military strength or the psychological predisposition to go farther afield than this.

And even territorial expansion was still seen largely in terms of personal aggrandizement. A despot extended his political influence as his situation permitted—through war, a lucky purchase, a fortunate marriage. The most sensational bid for wider authority during the Renaissance was made by one ruler of Milan, Gian Galeazzo Visconti. Late in the 14th Century Visconti, a Milanese aristocrat, gained control of nearly all Lombardy, the greater part of Tuscany and a number of cities in the Papal States. He was on the point of crushing Florence when suddenly he died. Yet Visconti did not think of this domain as a state so much as a collection of personal properties: in his will, he divided it among his children.

Nevertheless the Italian people had not forgotten that once upon a time their whole country had been unified. Their regional dialects might look different in print, but they were all versions of one language. During the 14th Century, when the Italians' interest in antiquity quickened, this consciousness increased. They became aware not only of a former unity, but of a common heritage of political greatness and cultural achievement. Cities took pride in their origin as Roman colonies or military camps. And however fierce the antagonisms between their governments, all Italians believed that the civilization they had in common was far superior to most others. Like their ancestors they looked upon most non-Italians as *barbari*, barbarians.

For the most part, however, these links with ancient Rome were seen as a cause for pride, not as a call to action. Only once did a Renaissance ruler attempt to bring the Roman Empire back to life. In 1347 Cola di Rienzo, a young Roman notary, seized the Roman government and resurrected for himself the old Roman title of Tribune of the People. Calling himself Champion of Italy and Friend of the World, he invited the rest of Italy to join him in a federation of states. But the peninsula was too faction-ridden to subscribe to a central government, and Rienzo was too hectic a visionary to be taken seriously. The Florentine historian Giovanni

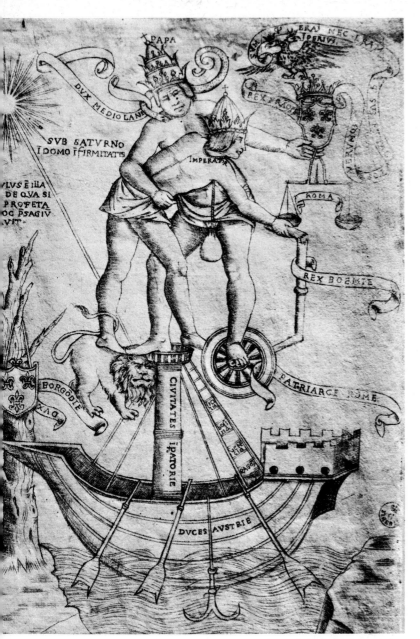

A FAMOUS POLITICAL MEETING *between Pope Paul II and the Holy Roman Emperor Frederick III is memorialized in this intricate allegory. Each element had meaning to 15th Century Italians; though no one can be certain today, the symbols were probably read this way: The Pope has a snake around his neck to symbolize the hostility of Milan, but he is supported by his authority as Patriarch of Rome, represented by the wheel on which his foot rests. The Emperor stands on a lion, symbol of his ally, Burgundy. Both have a foot on the ship of state (the Empire), the Emperor for obvious reasons, the Pope because he had power over parts of it. The steps by which Paul consolidated his position as Pope are noted on the rungs of the ladder. The moneybag dangling from the Emperor's neck is a reminder of his ambition and avarice.*

Villani, recording that "Rienzo wanted to bring all Italy under the obedience of Rome in the way of long ago," added a significant comment: "The enterprise was fantastic and could not endure."

The Italians are not an idealistic people. Their strongest feelings are reserved for the world they can see—for their families, for the town where they were born and its surrounding countryside. Even today, to be a native of Milan or Venice or Bologna means more to the average Italian than to be a native of Italy. To Renaissance Italians, "Italy" meant even less. It was a word that stood for something in battle, a rallying concept to use against French and Spanish enemies. But it did not conjure up a picture of Italian lions and lambs lying down together when peace was resumed. Alliances were formed to preserve the status quo, not transform it. To a friend who once wrote suggesting that the Italian states form a union to guard themselves against the ambitions of France and Spain, Machiavelli penned a tart reply: "Don't make me laugh."

The only common policy among the Italian states was an agreement to differ, and during the course of the Renaissance their differences became very marked. Earlier, in the Middle Ages, the most common form of government had been the republican commune, a voluntary organization of the merchants who had actually created the city—as a cluster of shops within or near the protecting shadow of a cathedral or monastery or some feudal lord's castle. In those days the offices of government were held by responsible men elected by their fellow citizens, members of the city's merchant class.

But with rising prosperity society became more complex, subdividing into many more economic and social groups. Tension developed between these groups, which led to conflict, which in turn led to deadlocks that could be resolved only by turning over the power of state to one man. Thus arose the despots, the *signori*, men who were called in—or who stepped in—to deal with an emergency and found it convenient not to leave. By the middle of the 15th Century this practice was so general that there were few genuine republics left. And in only one of these did republican government survive without diminution or interruption.

Venice, isolated by its lagoons and untroubled by any political or territorial commitments on the mainland until the 14th Century, had concentrated all its attention on its overseas trade. Venetian ships handled much of the pilgrim traffic to the Holy Land; Venetian agents bought up Indian spices, carpets, damasks and jewels in Alexandria and Beirut, wood and furs from Scandinavia, wool from England, cloth from Flanders, and wine from France. With an empire of trading posts in the Aegean and the Levant, it had become the richest and at the same time the least Italian of the Italian city-states. Its bazaars were a cosmopolitan bustle to which all nationalities were welcome: few places had less prejudice against Jews, and even Moslem infidels were free to buy and sell there.

This open-minded pursuit of the ducat made Venice rich and aroused the envy of the rest of Christendom, for the riches were not concealed. The piles on which the city was built groaned under the weight of the palaces of its merchant princes. In 1495 a French ambassador, Philippe de Commines, reported: "the houses are very large and lofty, and built of stone; the old ones are all painted, those of about a hundred years standing are faced with white marble from Istria . . . and inlaid with porphyry and serpentine. Within they have, most of them . . . rich marble chimney-pieces, bedsteads of gold color, their portals of the same, and most gloriously furnished. In short, it is the most triumphant city that I have ever seen, the most respectful to all ambassadors and strangers, governed with the greatest wisdom, and serving God with the most solemnity."

THE ARSENAL IN VENICE *is depicted in this animated print. The Italian legend explains that beyond this gate "galleys and other war vessels are made continually, and these people whom you see are the workmen." The second caption reads: "Here the workmen are paid." This state-run shipyard became the largest industrial complex of the Renaissance, employing thousands of workers and using production methods that presaged the modern assembly line.*

This solemnity was displayed in a specifically Venetian manner. The city's religious processions were as much civic as ecclesiastical ceremonies; officers of state paced, soberly gorgeous, among the representatives of religious orders. And the most splendid of Venetian churches, San Marco, was not its cathedral, but the private chapel of the doge, the head of the Venetian state.

The state, in fact, played a unique role in the whole life of Venice. It not only dominated the Church, but it owned the largest industrial enterprise, the Arsenal, an enormous dockyard. It leased the Arsenal's galleys to individual merchants. And although each merchant's business was a matter of his own private initiative, Venetian trade as a whole was subject to state planning. It was the state that distributed licenses for overseas trade, the state that determined the routes and times of sailing for the six trade convoys which left Venice annually—one to Greece and Constantinople; one to the Black Sea; one each to Syria, Egypt, the north coast of Africa; and one to England and Flanders. Regulations were designed to prevent any licensee from becoming too rich and to save any who were in danger of going bankrupt.

The Venetian capitalist accepted these measures because he had come to think of his personal interests as bound up with those of the state. The state's navy patrolled the sea lanes along which his cargoes moved; its diplomats negotiated the treaties through which he obtained goods from distant, sometimes hostile, lands. The taxes imposed on him were imposed by men whose concerns were identical to his own, for the government was composed of men like himself.

Citizenship in the Venetian republic was restricted to the men of some 200 patrician families. Together these men formed the Great Council, the base of the governmental pyramid. The Council elected the members of the Senate, the chief legis-lative body, and also, directly or indirectly, the members of the much smaller executive body, the Collegio (or cabinet) as well as the doge and his six councillors.

The symmetry of this pyramid was complicated by one additional organ of government, the Council of Ten, elected annually by the Great Council to handle emergencies involving the safety of the state. The Ten provided the speed, and the lifetime dogeship the continuity, that enabled Venice to meet external crises without becoming involved in internal crises as well. Other states reacted to the shock of wars and financial disaster by firing their leaders or tinkering with their forms of government. But the Venetian government continued to function in even the most calamitous times. It could not have done so, however, without the existence of still another factor: the strong sense of unity that bound together the entire population.

Unlike other Italian cities, Venice had no old landed aristocracy to absorb into its new merchant class. Although the members of the Great Council thought of themselves proudly as nobility, they had for generations engaged in trade and saw nothing demeaning in it. As merchants they understood the artisans and craftsmen with whom they had business dealings, and were shrewd enough to include them in the religious and patriotic festivals that were a feature of Venetian life. There were no political assassinations in Venice, no proletarian revolts, and comparatively little of the group rivalry that plagued the decision-making procedures of other republican cities.

Ironically, however, Venice's successful republicanism had less influence on the founders of later constitutional governments than the Renaissance republics that failed. It was the sense of failure, and the attendant heart-searching, that provided the beginnings of modern political thought. It was not Venice in its greatness, but Florence in its decline that produced Machiavelli, the most original political thinker of the Renaissance. Machiavelli was concerned not with celebrating victory, but with analyzing the causes of defeat. His city, unlike Venice, was not of one economic mind, and antagonism between its classes was much sharper.

In Florence, banking and industry, as well as trade, were strongly developed businesses and Florentine businessmen at times pulled against each other. They were also prey to internal strains. Manufacturers were exposed to the threat of foreign competition and the vagaries in price and availability of raw materials, especially of wool for the textile industry. Bankers loaned money to foreign princes on such uncertain collateral as next year's taxes, subjecting the stability of their firms to forces outside their control. To these problems were added the unexpected strains of disasters such as the Black Death, which in the mid-14th Century wiped out half the labor force vital to Florentine industry. (Venice, too, was affected but, relying less on labor, was left comparatively better off.)

But the factor which toppled most of the commune-republics and produced periodic convulsions in those that survived was the combat between different classes. All of them were trying to make the most of the economic advantages of urban life, and some, in addition, were trying to maintain the prestige earned through dignified birth. The latter were descendants of the old feudal nobility, men whose taste for fighting and scorn of mere citizens had not been entirely dulled by long residence in towns.

In the second half of the 15th Century the caste-consciousness of this group was intensified. This was partly because rulers like the kings of Naples and the Sforza despots of Milan were increasingly satisfying their military leaders with grants of land and using men of the noble class, rather than middle-class professionals, to administer their outlying possessions. In the republics it was the affluent and

"MOUTHS OF TRUTH" *decorated the façades of government buildings in Venice. The mouths of the masks were slots into which Venetians dropped denunciations of suspected criminals. The head above was for "secret denunciations of smugglers"; the one below for unmasking bribers and grafters—"anyone who conceals gifts or remunerations." If an accusation proved false, the informer was fined.*

leisured middle class that intensified class-consciousness—by admiring the chivalrous aristocracy whose tastes and manners did not smack of the countinghouse.

Then there was the commercial class, itself divided by rivalry between family groups and by antagonism between established families and the "new men." The former had built up the economic fortunes of the state and formed a patrician group; the latter continually broke into their charmed circle through business enterprise or wealthy marriage. Members of this employer class were known as *popolo grasso*, the "fat men." Below them were the "little people," the *popolo minuto*, composed of shopkeepers, craftsmen, notaries and merchants with small family businesses. Lowest of all, and largest in number, were the unskilled or semiskilled workers—largely illiterate—who storm into the pages of history only in moments of revolt.

We know least about this largest class. We have no letter from a Renaissance workingman, no diary, no monument to his memory. From baptismal records we may find his name; from marriage registers, whom he married; from hospital records, what he died of. But the man himself remains silent. Many, perhaps most, of his number lived very near the subsistence level. Except for a brief period between 1378 and 1382, when the Florentine woolworkers revolted and won a voice in the government, he had no official organization and no political force. He was not allowed to form guilds to protect himself against his masters. He was a beast of burden driven by a society which at every level was interested only in making a profit out of his labors.

Apart from the decades of underpopulation that followed the Black Death in 1348, the continual immigration of peasants into the city meant that there was always unemployment. Workers could not afford to strike. They could not even exert pressure by refusing to serve in the army, since most governments relied not on citizen soldiers but on hired professionals. Any attempt to combine in protest against working conditions was quickly detected by the merchant and shopkeeper guilds, and punished.

Except by serving as a mercenary, it was virtually impossible for a poor man to better his condition. He might be favored by a commander for bravery in battle, but in industry he was ignored. Patrician merchants spoke of having their sons learn the business from the bottom up, but the bottom was the front of the shop, not the factory floor. The presence of the proletariat can be felt in literary references to the wit and ingenuity of the common man, and its pressure upon events can be sensed from the references to politicians wooing the people in moments of crisis. But it cannot be seen as a calculable force.

The same cannot be said for the other three groups—the nobility, the *popolo grasso* and the *popolo minuto*. Their efforts to affect the course of public affairs reduced the governments of most republics to political confusion. In Siena, for instance, by 1355, the nobles had been excluded from public affairs and the city was governed by a group of rich bankers and merchant-industrialists, the upper middle class. Then, in that same year, following a number of bank failures, this group was replaced by a government of *middle*-middle-class citizens: judges, notaries and physicians. By 1369, through a series of revolts, power had passed to the lower middle class—small merchants and thriving artisans. In 1371 another revolt, aimed at moving power still lower in the social scale, failed. It was followed by 14 years of minor crises until finally, in 1385, the administration was more or less stabilized through an uneasy coalition of all three middle classes.

In Genoa a similar pattern of internal confusion was complicated still more by outside interference.

Genoa was coveted by Milan as a sea outlet for its commerce, and by France as a port of entry to the Italian peninsula in time of war; at various periods during the Renaissance, Genoa was forced to accept the suzerainty of one or another of the two powers.

Beginning in 1499 the city was ruled for nearly a decade by a French governor, with the support of the Genoese aristocracy. The *popolo grasso*, whose loss of political power should logically have forced them into an alliance with the *popolo minuto*, hesitated, partly out of distaste for the lower middle class, partly out of sympathy with the aristocratic way of life. In hesitating, they lost the chance to regain a dominant role in the government. Instead the *popolo minuto* and the workers took the initiative and attempted a revolt that failed bloodily in 1507. Thereafter Genoa was ruled by its aristocracy and was only nominally a republic.

All over Italy by the middle of the 16th Century, the merchant commune had all but disappeared. Tradesmen no longer put up their shutters for the afternoon to go and sit in some council of state. The great bell of Florence no longer summoned Florentine citizens to give their assent to a change in government. States were ruled by princes and dominated by aristocratic courts whose members were occasionally of ancient noble birth, but more often were "aristocratized" merchants. It seemed almost as though the feudal lord of the Middle Ages had, as it were, bided his time, ridden out the "democratic" storms and returned in triumph, armed with a balance sheet rather than a lance.

In leaving behind their age of rowdy experiment, the Italians also left behind one of history's great testing periods of government of and by the people. The republics had their flaws: their ruling bodies, with membership terms of usually no more than six months, lacked continuity; their appointments, made by election and lot, often put unqualified men into important positions. But for all their faults these governments had offered unrivaled opportunities. The average Italian was more likely to play a part in guiding the fortunes of his state than his contemporaries elsewhere. And the state, because of its smallness, gave him a unique introduction into public affairs. Bombarded with a constant stream of political crises and constitutional experiments, he was, for his time, the best-trained political animal in Europe.

Similarly, Italy's head start into capitalism—into an economy based on money-wealth rather than the ownership of land—enabled its merchants and bankers to survive the economic depressions and epidemics of plague that swept Europe in the 14th and 15th Centuries. Capitalistic practices, with their greater complexity, made Italian businessmen at first more vulnerable to these catastrophes. But in the end their broadly based economic skills equipped them to recover. They invented better bookkeeping methods, learned to use the cushion of diversification, arranged more flexible credit facilities, streamlined and subdivided work processes to cut down costs and raise production.

But Italians were not only more astute politically and economically than their European fellow men; they were also better educated. From the public interest shown in art to the scorn heaped in popular literature upon stupid country yokels, it is apparent that the Italians as a people cared about learning, and were interested in many matters beyond those immediately involved in earning a living. Artisans paid attention to the changing political and financial fortunes of their vigorous, gossiping cities; intellectuals, observing the whole peninsula, were acutely conscious of its varying governments and methods of doing business. The endless shades of difference in Italian civic life powerfully affected all its citizens, stimulating each man to bring his talents, whether for art or business, into the open —to be sharpened by competition.

A CITY OF SHIPS, *Venice was a center of travel during the Renaissance. It was a starting point for many pilgrimages, by sea and over land.*

A RENAISSANCE JOURNEY

Any journey was a hazardous venture in Renaissance Italy. Travelers often carried their own luggage, took potluck at the public inns, risked run-ins with the armed brigands who loitered along the roads. A long trip, one wayfarer said, required "the back of an ass, the belly of a hog and a conscience as broad as the king's highway." Nevertheless, merchants regularly traveled throughout Italy, while pilgrims from the far corners of Europe flocked to Rome, the capital of Christendom. The pictures that follow retrace a trip from Venice to Rome, with all the wonders and pitfalls characteristic of the time and the place.

MOORED GONDOLAS, *at the entrance of Venice's Grand Canal, bob behind a stone lantern. During the Renaissance, the city was filled with some 10,000 gondolas—more than serve Venice now.*

THE SUMPTUOUS, FLOATING WORLD OF VENICE

Venice was a natural place to begin a long journey, for the Venetians were among Italy's most travel-minded people, and Renaissance tourists besieged the city. For the host of visiting pilgrims, merchants, artists and adventurers, special guides were available to point out the sights and see that innocents were not fleeced in the shops. From canopied gondolas *(right)*, travelers gaped at the hundreds of Byzantine palaces shimmering above the water, at the great market square, the huge arsenal and glassworks—and at the women with their painted faces, low-cut gowns and high-heeled shoes.

Leaving this gilded, opulent city, travelers setting out on the long overland journey toward Rome outfitted themselves for the rigors of the road with broad hats, boots, breeches, gloves—and extra pairs of overalls for nights spent in dirty public inns.

VENETIAN BOATERS *take gondolas along the Grand Canal, as pedestrians use sidewalks on its banks. This 15th Century work by Vittore Carpaccio shows the old Rialto drawbridge over the canal.*

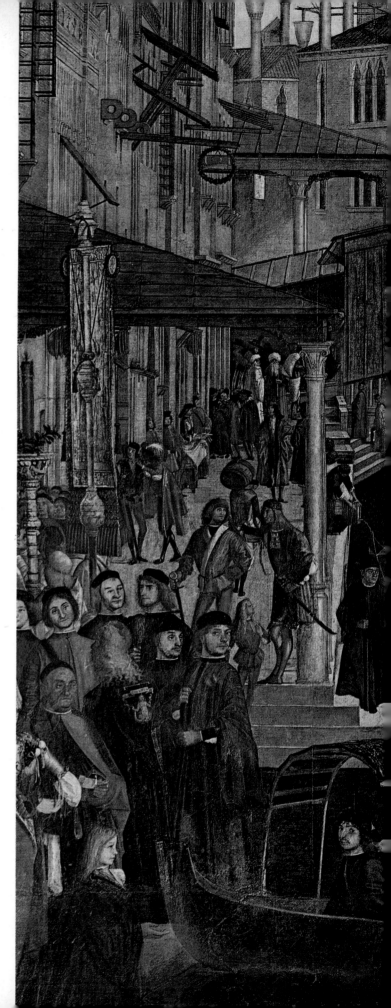

THE PASTORAL BEAUTY OF THE PO VALLEY

Outside Venice, the way to Rome took travelers through the broad, flat Po River Valley. Crossing this fertile terrain of farmlands, meadows, orchards, vineyards and woods, wayfarers could glance back at the distant ridges of the Alps. Ahead lay the Apennines, and then Florence. This luxuriant valley, called the garden of Italy, seemed like a cornucopia: it poured forth fruits, flowers and vegetables in such abundance that one weary pilgrim said a first view "did . . . tickle my senses with inward joy."

UMBRELLA PINES *etch delicate shapes against the sky. These trees, celebrated by Renaissance poets, are still landmarks of the Italian countryside.*

A ROADSIDE VENDOR *offers fruits to wayfarers in a painting by Vincenzo Campi. Vendors set up stands outside towns to avoid paying tolls on their produce at the town gate.*

A LABORIOUS ASCENT *faced travelers as they left the Po Valley for the foothills of the Apennines. The trip from Venice to Florence, about 150 miles, took as long as two weeks.*

A WAYSIDE BATH *in a country stream refreshes travelers, in this painting by Bernardino Luini, a follower of Leonardo da Vinci. Pilgrims stopped at streams famous for their curative powers.*

A SKYLINE IN STONE, *the profile of Florence featured the central Duomo, Giotto's marble belltower to its left and a medieval city hall, at right.*

A DOMED SHOWPIECE, *the Duomo dominated Florence. Michelangelo said that he could construct a dome "bigger, yes, but not more beautiful."*

FLORENCE: NOBLE HOME FOR A VITAL PEOPLE

Seeing Florence from the surrounding sandstone hills, a 15th Century traveler from Venice sensed a great difference in the two cities. In contrast to the watery splendor and gaiety of Venice, Florence revealed itself in severe towers and austere buildings. Most imposing was the great cathedral *(left)*.

A traveler who lingered in Florence found the people an enigmatic breed. On the streets of the city, illiterate workmen went about singing verses from Dante's *Divine Comedy*. High culture was a part of everyday life, yet Florence was also a city of down-to-earth, fast-talking merchants—gifted, as people said, with "sharp eyes and pointed tongues."

CLOAKED TRAVELERS *stand on a streetcorner in Florence, looking for a night's lodging. All of the city's public inns were located on a single street, and their management was strictly regulated.*

A LONELY VILLA, *built during the Renaissance, occupies a rocky precipice above the Tessino Valley, outside Spoleto. A road on top of a Roman aqueduct took travelers across the ravine to the villa, which is now inaccessible.*

MARAUDING BRIGANDS, *a band of mercenary soldiers, stage a surprise attack upon two defenseless travelers outside a fortified town in a painting*

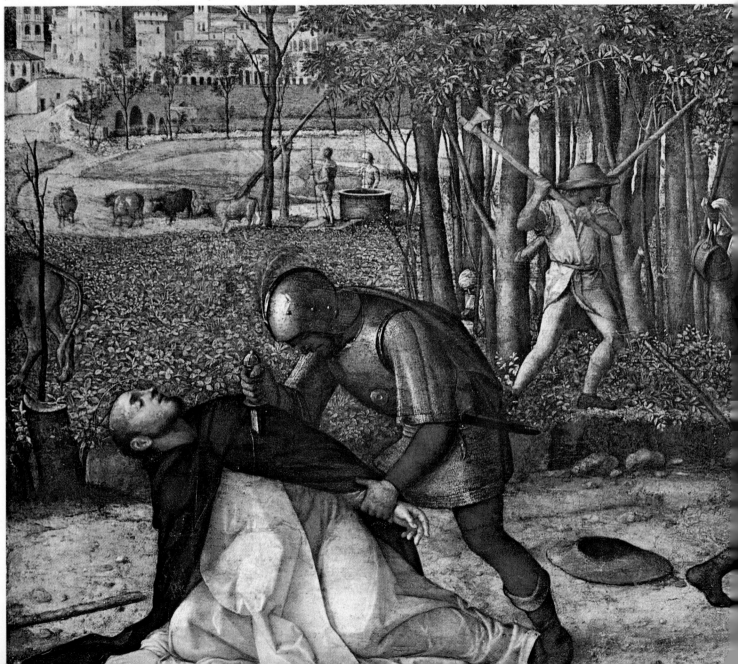

THE HAZARDS OF TRAVEL

Leaving Florence, Rome-bound travelers faced the most difficult and menacing leg of their journey. The ancient Roman roads that wound through the mountains were compounded of dust, loose stones and ruts; in wet weather they were so muddy that all progress was often halted.

But travelers preferred any physical hardship to an encounter with the notorious bandits and mercenaries who infested many hilltop towns and castles along the way. Although travelers hired armed escorts, the guards were seldom a match for the brigands. Those who were only robbed were fortunate. Many travelers were slaughtered or held for ransom. To avoid planned ambushes, merchants would loudly announce they were going one way and then quietly head in the opposite direction.

attributed to Giovanni Bellini. In the background woodcutters calmly continue about their jobs, accustomed to assaults and robberies along the road.

THE MIXED BLESSINGS OF A PUBLIC INN

After a day on the Italian roads, tired travelers counted on stopping overnight at monasteries or private homes. But if no such lodgings were available, the wayfarer took his chances at a public inn. Innkeepers often posted men along the highways, up to 20 miles away, to vie with competitors, praise their hostelries and even to carry the travelers' luggage. At the inns, mimes and fiddlers amused the guests. The lodgings were frequently dirty—and there was as much danger of robbery as on the roads. Yet travelers had to settle themselves before dark or fare as in a proverb of the time—"He who comes late has a poor supper and a worse bed."

A COUNTRY CASTLE, *Casale Marco Simone is located 15 miles from Rome. Pilgrims often stopped overnight at such estates.*

REQUESTING ROOMS *at a public inn, two road-weary pilgrims are introduced by a manservant to the innkeeper (far right) and his assistant.*

48

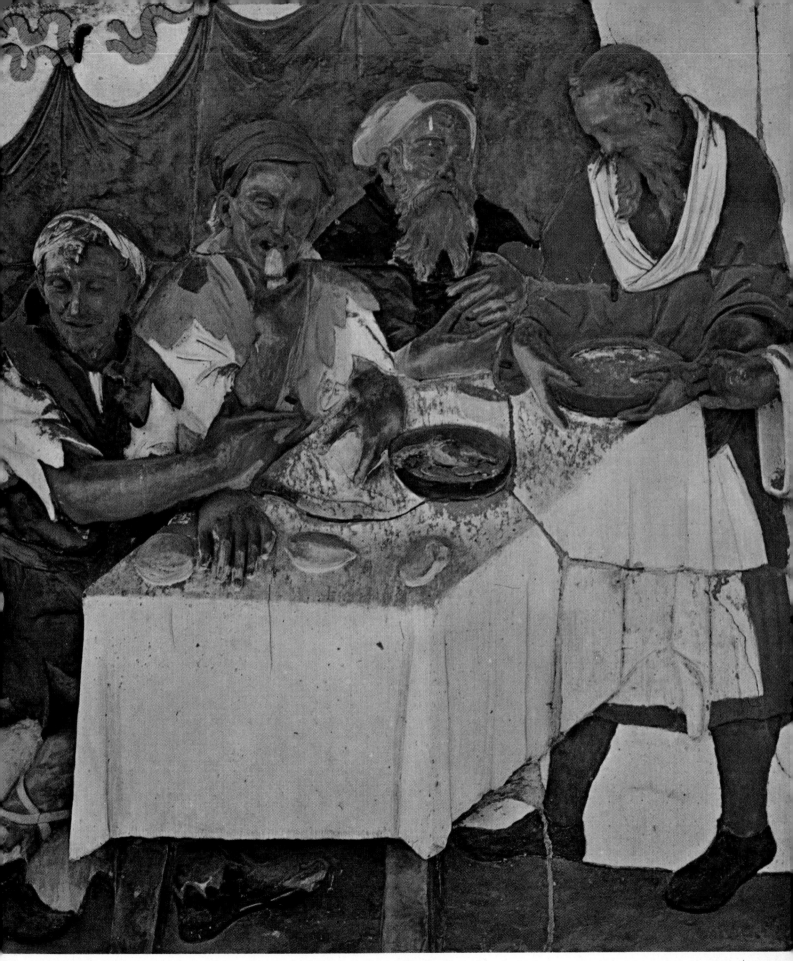

POOR WAYFARERS *receive a free meal at a monastery table. Monks offered shelter to all travelers; those of means were expected to make a donation.*

IN HOLY DRESS, *pilgrims gather in the costume traditional for pious travelers: a staff, a knapsack and a cap with scallop shells.*

ROME: THE PILGRIM'S ULTIMATE GOAL

Reaching Rome, travelers found a city of decaying buildings and rubble-filled streets. Sheep and goats grazed on the seven hills where emperors and senators once built temples and villas. Men with shovels and pickaxes were demolishing what was left of Rome's crumbling monuments to get marble for the manufacture of lime. In the shadow of ruined aqueducts, people drank the water of the Tiber.

Yet to the arriving pilgrims, the poet Petrarch said, Rome was a city "full of sacred bones and relics of the martyrs." Carrying religious guidebooks and a map *(opposite)* of the city's seven great churches, pilgrims followed a tour prescribed for the penitent. Each church offered some special grace. For example, entering one brought a pilgrim 48,000 years remittance of punishment for his sins.

THE SEVEN CHURCHES *of Rome are pictured on a map like those that*

In Herusalem

S. Sebastiano

S. PAVLO

S. GIOVANI LATRANO

S. PIETRO

Renaissance pilgrims carried with them. A long line of penitents winds past St. Peter's, in the foreground, the last stop on the customary tour.

3

MANNERS AND MORALS

It was Renaissance Italy that worked out the art of living in towns for the rest of Europe and for an increasingly urbanized posterity. The Italian town was more than a market or an administrative center; it was a place in which a man could pass his whole life, a place which provided a full round of employment and entertainment not only for a bourgeoisie with rising standards of comfort and culture, but for a nobility which elsewhere in Europe preferred to spend its time in aristocratic seclusion on its country estates.

The countryside, to the Italian citizen, was a place to visit. Many merchants and shopkeepers owned vineyards and olive groves, and left the city to live near them during the weeks of harvest; among the rich and powerful it became fashionable to have a country villa. It satisfied the growing taste for aristocratic pursuits such as hawking and hunting, and set the cachet of expensive leisure on a successful business or political career. The villas of the Medici at Cafaggiolo and Careggi, the retreat of the Sforzas at Vigévano, the Schifanoia estate of the dukes of Ferrara, were all holiday places. Real life, satisfactory life, lay in the towns. Princes, bankers and shopkeepers returned with pleasure from fields and woods that were certainly beautiful, and often profitable, but which they could not help regarding as a cultural wilderness populated by rustic barbarians.

It was for town dwellers that writers like Leon Battista Alberti and Matteo Palmieri, in the first half of the 15th Century, set down elaborate philosophies on the conduct of family life. These writers held that the home was the training ground for the virtues which made for a healthy state: thrift, moderation, a sense of public duty. The ideal family atmosphere should not direct children toward a life of scholarly seclusion or wealthy exclusiveness, but toward a responsible commitment to the state. Dignity and restraint in the home, public service outside it: this was the new bourgeois ideology. It took its place beside the only two codes of behavior the Middle Ages had known, the feudal knight's adherence to chivalry, the priest's or monk's life based on the discipline of religion.

This bourgeois ideal grew from the circumstances of making a living: a merchant had to appear trust-

A GIFT OF THE GUILDS, *Verrocchio's "Christ and St. Thomas" stands outside a 14th Century Florentine church—a building which had once been a grain market. The statue was presented in 1483 by the governor of the city's guilds.*

worthy, but at the same time be canny. It was saved from being an ideology of crass acquisitiveness by two things. One was the genuineness of the feeling that involvement in the life of the state was a necessity, since without state protection business would be impossible. The second was the propaganda of writers like Petrarch and Leonardo Bruni, who made bourgeois virtues respectable by associating them with the political and economic developments of ancient Rome.

Petrarch believed that the ideal man combined the opposing virtues of self-containment and public-spiritedness, but he never presented this view as more than a philosophical idea. It remained for Pier Paolo Vergerio, in 1404, to codify it into an educational system. In his treatise, *De ingenuis moribus* (On Good Manners), Vergerio insisted that the purpose of education was not merely to produce scholars, but to develop character and prepare children for a busy and competitive life in the world of men and affairs. These goals were quite unlike those of medieval teaching, which had concentrated on memorizing and acquiring specific kinds of knowledge.

The new educational aim was put into effect by the Renaissance's two most influential schoolmasters, Vittorino da Feltre and Guarino da Verona. Their schools—Vittorino's at Mantua and Guarino's at Ferrara—were originally opened for the children of the princely rulers of these cities, the Gonzaga and the Este. But Vittorino and Guarino subsequently accepted gifted poorer boys as well. Families from all over Italy competed to get their sons enrolled in the two schools, and thus the ideas of their founders affected other academies throughout the peninsula.

Vittorino believed in making learning attractive. He taught spelling and reading by using movable letters, and simple arithmetic by games. He also introduced his pupils to classical literature through stories and conversation about its content. Although there was some teaching from religious texts in the early grades, as the boys moved into the higher grades the literature of Rome, and to a lesser extent, of Greece, became the staples. For moral instruction Roman texts were frequently preferred over more modern works—because the Latin of pagan writers like Cicero and Seneca was purer than the Latin of some Christian scholars. Cicero was perhaps most important for his writings on rhetoric; persuasive speech was seen to be especially useful for boys who would become involved in public affairs. And to supplement these readings from ancient orators, pupils were often taken to hear contemporary political speeches or to listen to some famous lawyer pleading in the courts. The acquisition of learning, it was constantly stressed, was not only for ornament but for use.

The Renaissance belief that a study of Greek and Roman classics was the best training for the intelligence had a profound effect on later educators. In this respect, and in others, Vittorino's institution was the forerunner of the British public (and American private) school. Something of a stoic, he believed in a spartan environment. He thought that reading aloud was a better antidote to cold than a cozy fire. He saw the playing field as a catch basin for surplus energy and as a training ground for courage, discipline and cooperation. In addition to team games, Vittorino and Guarino encouraged riding and swimming. In one instance, Guarino urged on waverers by characteristically referring back to antiquity: "It is more important to remember how many illustrious persons have been good swimmers. Let it be enough to mention Horatius Cocles, Alexander and Caesar." Throughout history the knightly class had always been trained for war. But when Renaissance educators became aware that certain Roman military writers had emphasized the importance of the fitness of

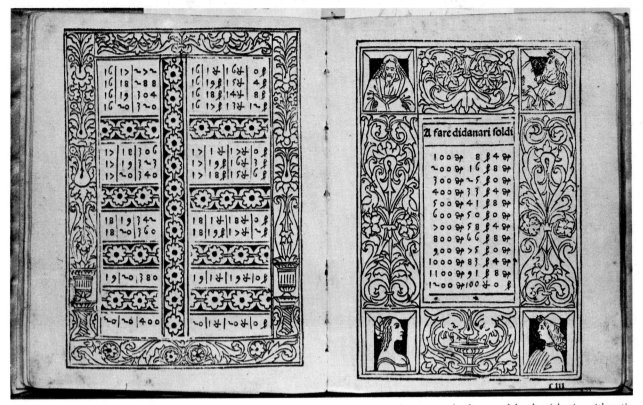

MATHEMATICS FOR MERCHANTS, *this copiously decorated book of basic arithmetic aided Renaissance tradesmen in making their everyday business calculations. At the left are multiplication tables; at right, a table of conversion for Florentine coins.*

ordinary soldiers, and when they learned of the emphasis put on athletics in the Greek states, they began to feel that physical training was important for their schools too. Muscular Christianity has a heritage of more than five hundred years.

Renaissance educators believed that the purpose of education was to turn out men equipped to fit knowledgeably, and with charm, into any walk of life. The emphasis on charm was again a product of urban environment: men had to move with ease and effectiveness· through a richly varied society. This led to a special preoccupation with the art of conversation, and to a conviction that one of the cardinal social sins was to be boring. A 16th Century book on social behavior denounces as "unpardonable . . . those people who can never talk of anything but their children, their wives, and their nursemaids," and "who take every opportunity to tell us of their dreams." Such scruples about boring conversation suggest that discussion must have

played a large part in Renaissance social gatherings, both formal and informal. And it did. The great number of books in dialogue form makes this clear—not so much classical literary models like the *Dialogues* of Plato, but a whole spate of Renaissance dialogues. By and large, Italians liked to talk and they were good at it.

From the lively and uninhibited role given to women in these dialogues, it might seem that the position of women improved appreciably during the Renaissance. In point of fact, with rare exceptions, it did not. The accident of inheritance or marriage threw into the limelight such intelligent and forthright women as Isabella d'Este and Caterina Sforza, the former to become one of the Renaissance's most passionate patrons of the arts, the latter to defend her city, Forlì, against Cesare Borgia with the vigor and ingenuity of a born soldier. But ordinary women were still expected to keep quiet and not display their learning or independence of mind. In the 14th Century a Florentine merchant could write: "Woman is a light thing and vain. . . . If you have women in your house, keep them shut up as much as possible and return home very often and keep them in fear and trembling." At the end of the 15th Century the Florentine bookseller Vespasiano da Bisticci, following two main rules for women enunciated by St. Paul, could say essentially the same thing: "The first is that they bring up their children in the fear of God, and the second that they keep quiet in church, and I would add that they stop talking in other places as well."

Vespasiano's comments were part of a huge literature devoted to good manners. Much of this was written to instruct newly rich people how to behave in order to enter the class above them; in other cases it defined an ideal upper-class personality and behavior, and was designed not so much to ease the entry of outsiders as to keep them out. The first behavior books, dating from the thriving commercial communes of the 13th Century, dealt with such basic matters as personal cleanliness and table manners. In about 1290, Fra Bonvincino da Riva's *The Fifty Courtesies for the Table*, points out that "he who gets mad drunk offends in three ways: he harms his body and soul, and he loses the wine which he consumes."

But as time went on, and the social structure hardened, there were fewer books dealing with such matters as spitting and scratching during meals, and more books on the general deportment of a whole class, especially the middle class. These books reflect a fear of those antagonisms which we have already noted as plaguing the political fortunes of the Italian cities, by stressing the need to be respectful to superiors and gracious to inferiors. They fitted into a carefully patterned civic life in which edicts regulated all sorts of matters: the goods of which clothes could be made, the value of ornaments women could wear, the number of

guests to invite to a banquet—even the type of plate (not too much silver or gold) on which the banquet (not too many courses) could be served. The purpose of this sumptuary legislation was partly spiritual; it reflected a lingering strain of medieval austerity. However it was also economic, to check the consumption of imported luxuries and thus foster home industries, and even political, to check ostentation and thus minimize class jealousies.

Perhaps the most influential of all the behavior books produced in the Italian Renaissance was Baldassare Castiglione's *The Courtier:* a record of a series of conversations which supposedly took place in 1507 at the court of Urbino. Its recommended attitudes and attainments were followed all over Europe. Castiglione took the humanist ideal of the worldly, broadly educated man and infused it with chivalric attitudes of loyalty to princes and courtesy to women. His book has the charm of mood and language that give it the universal passport of great literature.

But *The Courtier*, for all the glamorous portrait of its central character—the man of gracefully varied accomplishments—has its less attractive side. It is a class document, written by a gentleman for gentlemen, and particularly for those gentlemen who attend the court of a prince. Castiglione warns the courtier against cheapening himself by mixing too freely with inferiors. He should not wrestle with a peasant, for example, "unless he is assured of getting the upper hand." Mix with other classes he will have to do on occasion, but he should do it sparingly lest familiarity breed contempt; "for there is nothing so excellent in the world that the ignorant people have not their fill of, and smally regard it in often beholding it." He insists on nobility of birth as a prerequisite for a courtier: good men come from good families. The fact that the civilization of Italy had thrived on the mixed blood in its veins was a lesson Castiglione, in the stratified society of the early 16th Century—and in a little autocratic state—could not afford to observe.

He spoke then for a small class at the top, ignoring the fact that one cannot speak for a class and for an unrestricted individualism at the same time. In contrast to the behavior books of the 15th Century, which took the family as the center from which a man looks outward to service with the state, *The Courtier* took the court as the center and looked upward to a prince. Its ideal man made himself dependent on the court and its ruler. In fact, Castiglione was not describing the ideal man but the ideal courtier, and sometimes the two came in conflict. For the courtier it was important not only to know his own worth, but to proclaim it by discreet advertisement. He should be careful to ride near the front in processions, else people would become too bored to notice him. In battle he should try to bring off his most daring feats of arms under the eye of the prince, regardless of their effect upon the battle plan as a whole.

Castiglione's courtier was also open to the charge of insincerity. He was expected to adjust himself to any company, always to show himself to the best advantage, to know himself, but to exploit that knowledge to impress people. When offered a favor or honor, he should pretend to refuse—but in such a way that he would be offered it again, more pressingly. He should conceal some of his special talents so that, when the moment came to display them, their effect would have the added charm of surprise. There is a very strong element of gamesmanship in *The Courtier*.

Fundamental to the book is the notion of *sprezzatura*, an easy nonchalance. Nothing should be done doggedly, with strain. The cult of accomplished amateurism, which influenced well-bred behavior for centuries, began with Castiglione's celebration of it. Into a world of political disaster and economic decline, a world which needed an increased profes-

RULES FOR GOOD CONDUCT

"GALATEO," or "The Book of Manners," extracts from which appear below, was published in 1558 and soon won international acceptance. The author, Giovanni della Casa, named the work "Galateo" after a fellow cleric famed for his probity.

Everyone should dress well, according to his age and his position in society. If he does not, it will be taken as a mark of contempt for other people.

Anyone whose legs are too thin, or exceptionally fat, or perhaps crooked, should not wear vivid or parti-colored hose, in order not to attract attention to his defects.

Refrain as far as possible from making noises which grate upon the ear, such as grinding or sucking your teeth.

A man . . . will take care not to get his fingers so greasy as to dirty his napkin with them, because the sight of it would be unsavory to others. Nor is it polite to wipe them on the bread.

Wit should be like the nibble of a sheep rather than the bite of a dog, for if it were to bite like a dog it would not be witty but insulting.

You should beware of coarseness in any form, because however amusing such things may seem to be, honorable people should only use honorable means of pleasing others.

A man should never boast of his birth, his honors or his wealth, and still less of his brains . . . as many people do.

You must talk neither too slowly, as though you had lost your taste for speech, nor too avidly, as though you were ravenous for it, but composedly as a sober man should.

A man must . . . not be content to do things well, but must also aim to do them gracefully.

sionalism, needed dour single-minded experts in government or finance, he introduced the ideal of the dilettante—and the dilettante not just as ornament to the court but as adviser to the prince. For *The Courtier* is not merely a book about refined behavior; it is also an attempt to correct the defects in the conduct of state affairs. Castiglione shared the general concern about Italy's problems—especially the endemic ones of war and diplomacy—with other thoughtful men of his generation. He believed in the idea of princely governments, but recognized that some princes lacked ability. His courtier was a man whose rounded personality, self-possession and charm would make the prince turn to him for advice. It is a persuasive notion until put against the trenchant common sense of Machiavelli, who wrote in *The Prince:* "It is an infallible rule that a prince who is not wise himself cannot be well advised."

As a contribution to political thought, Castiglione's work was naive. And so, perhaps, was its attempt to improve society. *The Courtier*—and for that matter all the behavior books—was written against a background of violence and insecurity, of lawlessness in ill-lit streets, of murder, bloody riots and open prostitution. Castiglione sought to bridle this lawlessness by advocating a calm demeanor and good manners. Other writers attacked the problem frontally. In the *Book of Good Examples and Good Manners*, the 14th Century Florentine Paolo di Pace da Certaldo warns his readers: "Beware of going out of your house at night, but if you are obliged to go, then take a trusty companion with you, and a large and good light. If you go to any dangerous place, go without telling anyone where you are going. In like manner, if you are going to Siena, say you are going to Lucca and you will be safe from evil people."

The very entertainments were violent. Broken limbs were a commonplace in the tournaments and mock fights that were popular diversions in city squares, and even death was not unusual. It was a time of savage torture, of public manglings of criminals; more than one chronicler describes pickup football games played with the heads of executed prisoners of war. Combats between wild beasts were a popular spectacle, and so were less brutal but more lascivious displays. When on one such occasion in Florence, a stallion was loosed in a group of mares, some of the tens of thousands of spectators were indignant, but one diarist wrote that "this was the most marvelous entertainment for girls."

It is impossible today to stage certain Renaissance comedies—like Machiavelli's *Mandragola*, for instance—with the frankness of the original. Lorenzo de' Medici himself wrote obscene carnival songs, and fresco painters decorated the palaces of great patrons with scenes that would raise most modern eyebrows.

From this climate of violence and refinement, of coarseness and reserve, two literary strains emerged. One was a worldly, secular literature urging men to heed the restraining counsels of the Church; the other was a satirical literature of protest against the courtly way of life, which was thought to be mincing and hypocritical. An example of the latter was a work called *The Courtesan*, by Pietro Aretino, the most energetic pornographer of the day, and designed as a satire on *The Courtier. The Courtesan* is a play about a foolish Sienese gentleman, Messer Maco, who goes to Rome to become a cardinal and win a fine mistress. He falls in love almost immediately with a girl at a window, and reflects that if only he were a courtier he could win her. Up comes a charlatan who says he is a master of courtiership and proceeds to give Messer Maco a lesson out of his textbook, a work on courtly behavior. The lessons—on how to deceive, how to flatter and how to employ hours in front of the looking glass—are, of

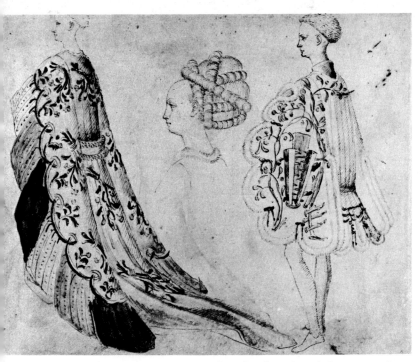

EXTRAVAGANT STYLES *adopted in the early 15th Century are shown in this sketch of elegant menswear and a feminine coiffure. The woman's hair is plucked to produce a fashionable high forehead.*

course, a gross mockery of the advice of Castiglione.

At the opposite pole is Giovanni della Casa's *Galateo*, written in the 1550s, which comes out for the euphemism rather than the frank word: "It is more fitting to speak of a lady's 'favorite' than of her 'lover'. . . . Again, when you are speaking to a woman or even to a man of gentle breeding, it is more polite to . . . speak of prostitutes as 'women of the world' than call them by their proper name." Taking exception to a long tradition of scurrilous anticlerical stories, Della Casa holds that "nothing must ever be said against God or the saints, either seriously or in jest, however witty and amusing it may be." Then, as a final stroke of compromise between what the individual feels to be right, and what the world expects of him, Della Casa observes, "We must subscribe not necessarily to the best customs, but to those which prevail in our day, just as we obey laws which may be far from good until the government, or whoever has the power to do so, has changed them."

But it is not entirely fair to contrast the "good" Della Casa with the "bad" Aretino. In his youth Della Casa wrote licentious verse that barred him from obtaining high office in the Church; and Are-

tino, for all his pagan enjoyment of the senses, was also the author of some moving and obviously sincere devotional works. The fact was that men could be both pious and dissolute at the same time, could admire both the sensual teaching of antiquity and the ascetic message of the Christian cloister.

For these and other reasons there was a conflict between humanism and Christianity, but it was not dramatic or critical. Men recognized that pagan learning and philosophy might undermine Christian faith, but the danger was not an alternative, or rival, faith. Rather, it was the possibility of the substitution of worldly for spiritual values. Religion, in fact, possibly played a larger part in everyday life than before. Between 1200 and 1550 Italy produced over 200 saints. No doubt this was more the result of effective lobbying at the Vatican than an increase in piety. Nevertheless, it did help to keep the Christian drama compelling by admitting to its cast a swelling list of local actors. There were also more bishoprics in Italy than in the rest of Western Christendom put together. And the clergy made up a greater proportion of the population.

Monasteries might be in a state of decay, and their membership in decline, but this was due, in part at least, to a concentration on extramonastic activities, on preaching and missionary work. The religious revivalism that flourished in Florence between 1494 and 1497 under the leadership of the fiery Dominican friar, Savonarola, was not an isolated phenomenon. Preachers up and down the peninsula had launched campaigns like his during the previous two centuries, attracting huge congregations and encouraging the burning of "vanities"—cosmetics, jewelry, false hair, indecent songs and pictures.

In the universities and convent schools the study of theology and canon law continued to prosper alongside the humanist education program. But now the teaching of the church was not necessar-

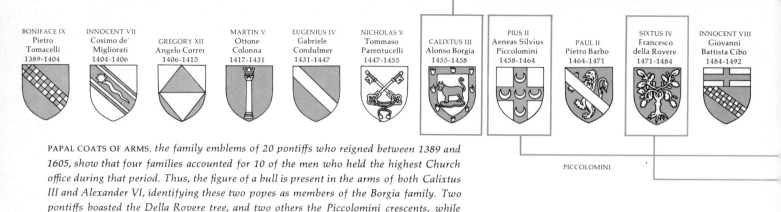

BONIFACE IX
Pietro
Tomacelli
1389-1404

INNOCENT VII
Cosimo de'
Migliorati
1404-1406

GREGORY XII
Angelo Correr
1406-1415

MARTIN V
Ottone
Colonna
1417-1431

EUGENIUS IV
Gabriele
Condulmer
1431-1447

NICHOLAS V
Tommaso
Parentucelli
1447-1455

CALIXTUS III
Alonso Borgia
1455-1458

PIUS II
Aeneas Silvius
Piccolomini
1458-1464

PAUL II
Pietro Barbo
1464-1471

SIXTUS IV
Francesco
della Rovere
1471-1484

INNOCENT VIII
Giovanni
Battista Cibo
1484-1492

PICCOLOMINI

PAPAL COATS OF ARMS, *the family emblems of 20 pontiffs who reigned between 1389 and 1605, show that four families accounted for 10 of the men who held the highest Church office during that period. Thus, the figure of a bull is present in the arms of both Calixtus III and Alexander VI, identifying these two popes as members of the Borgia family. Two pontiffs boasted the Della Rovere tree, and two others the Piccolomini crescents, while four displayed the most famous Renaissance crest—the six balls of the house of Medici.*

ily of a kill-joy nature. San Bernardino of Siena, one of the most popular preachers of the 15th Century, praised the joyous acceptance of life as intensely as any humanist. He also encouraged his congregations to "speak" with the Fathers of the Church, Augustine and Gregory, as intimately as Petrarch, in his letters, had "spoken" across the centuries to Cicero. Attached to the churches and monasteries, moreover, were thriving guilds of lay brothers, secular organizations for which a lively, popular devotional literature was produced in the vernacular.

To ordinary people throughout Italy religion in the Renaissance still played much the same role —and provoked the same responses—as it had in the Middle Ages. The diary of Luca Landucci, a Florentine apothecary who was a contemporary of Savonarola, describes the part played in the city's life by a miraculous painting of the Virgin in the neighboring town of Impruneta. On May 30, 1483, Landucci notes that "Our Lady of Impruneta was brought into the city, for the sake of obtaining fine weather, as it had rained for more than a month. And it immediately became fine." Again, on February 17, 1499: "The tabernacle of Our Lady of Impruneta was sent for, to enable us to decide whether it would be to our advantage to join the League and leave the King of France." When Landucci's idol, Savonarola, is excommunicated and his followers forbidden to hear him preach, the apothecary reluctantly follows the orthodox line: "Many did not go for fear of being excommunicated, saying

giusta vel ingiusta, temenda est (fair or unfair, we must take heed). I was one of those who did not go."

Yet alongside this vigorous religious life there was much anticlerical feeling. Priests were mocked for their ignorance, monks chided for sloth and immorality, prelates and popes condemned for putting cash and politics before the life of the spirit. The very number of the clergy, and the nonproductive nature of their work, made them the obvious butts of an intensely business-minded people. Furthermore, the Renaissance popes, although there is no cause to doubt their own private religious devotion, were disastrous leaders for a church in grave need of reform. Sixtus IV pushed his nephews into key positions; Innocent VIII shamelessly acknowledged his illegitimate children. The Vatican teemed with scandals under Alexander VI; and Julius II donned a warrior's armor to lead a papal army against local despots in Perugia and Bologna. Leo X loved magnificence and sold church offices to fill his treasury. Men despaired of reform coming from the top.

Then, in 1494, one man, troubled by the worldliness of popes and the vested interests of cardinals and bishops, set out to fight the battle alone. Savonarola proposed to make the city of Florence so holy that its example would spread to the rest of the Church. His experiment lasted three years, and in that three years Florence was in his power. Huge crowds jammed the churches when he preached and vice squads of boys and girls toured the streets,

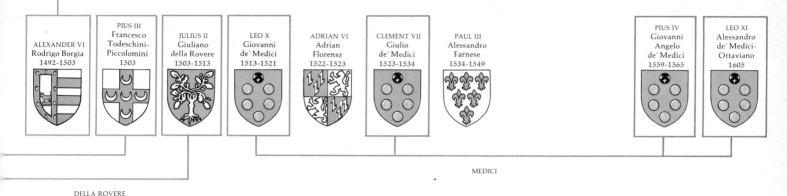

| ALEXANDER VI
Rodrigo Borgia
1492-1503 | PIUS III
Francesco
Todeschini-
Piccolomini
1503 | JULIUS II
Giuliano
della Rovere
1503-1513 | LEO X
Giovanni
de' Medici
1513-1521 | ADRIAN VI
Adrian
Florensz
1522-1523 | CLEMENT VII
Giulio
de' Medici
1523-1534 | PAUL III
Alessandro
Farnese
1534-1549 | PIUS IV
Giovanni
Angelo
de' Medici
1559-1565 | LEO XI
Alessandro
de' Medici-
Ottaviano
1605 |

MEDICI

DELLA ROVERE

rebuking overdressed women and denouncing gamblers. Hymns took the place of bawdy songs, religious processions the place of tournaments, and worldly trinkets went up in the smoke of ritual bonfires. The Medici rulers had been expelled from the city and Christ was named king, with Savonarola as His spokesman. How did one man, and a friar at that, come to exert so much control over the shrewdest, wittiest, most hardheaded capital in Europe?

Part of the answer lies in the Florentines' abiding religiosity, which, among other things, made them temperamentally susceptible to Savonarola's formidable gift of prophecy. He had foreseen the deaths of Lorenzo the Magnificent and Pope Innocent VIII a year before they happened; he had also foretold the arrival of the French army in Florence and the expulsion of the Medici. In addition there was the appeal of his pulpit personality: his eloquence made men quake and long to be saved.

But Savonarola was far more than a missionary zealot; he was involved in temporal affairs. Florence attended his sermons to be informed about Italian political events and how Florence's own new and crucial constitutional experiment was progressing. Savonarola had lent his support to the political party that wanted to provide for a more broadly based government. He had been one of the new government's ambassadors to the invading French King, Charles VIII, at whose approach Piero de' Medici had fled. He was listened to as one in touch with great affairs on earth, as well as the will of heaven. His pulpit broadcast news as well as the promise of eternal life.

And the broadcast went out to all of Florence. Savonarola spoke to the poor, about their relief from taxes as well as from their sins. He spoke to those of the wealthy class who had supported the new constitution. His emphasis on the imminent revival of purity in the Church echoed the yearnings for reform which were felt by humanists. Finally, he flattered the patriotic pride of his congregation by saying that God had marked out Florence as His instrument because of the spiritual and intellectual pre-eminence of her citizens.

In setting about his campaign against luxury and immorality, Savonarola was helped by the hysteria that always attends the beginning of a revivalist movement, and by the basic puritanism of a bourgeois society. But the charm of self-sacrifice soon wore off. Men began to feel nostalgia for the old, self-indulgent days of the Medici. The new government, furthermore, was working well and did not need Savonarola's eloquence to keep it going. The French alliance, with which he was closely identified, was not bringing any positive advantages; and the papacy, which this alliance had alienated, was bringing pressure to bear upon Florentine business interests with branches in Rome. Soon the tide turned against the reformer. His political supporters fell away; his religious disciples were cowed by the fear of papal censures. The pro-Medici and the pleasure-loving, together with the ecclesiastics who had been offended by Savonarola's holier-than-thou attitude, trumped up charges of heresy against him, "proved" them, and had him hanged and burned.

The charges were false. Savonarola was not a heretic—he opposed the Pope and his co-religionists for the tepidness of their belief, not for its dogmatic content. In fact, his passion for reform was no more than an angry footnote to the story of Renaissance religious orthodoxy. For all the great changes in the arts and in business life that characterized the period, no one thought seriously of changing the Church—not even Savonarola. He had fulminated against moral laxness, but not against the basic tenets of Renaissance morality—against the use of the arts to arouse desire or to nourish personal vainglory, but not against the study of nature and even of the nude. No great works of art are known to have been destroyed on the vanity bonfires, and the whitewashing of certain frescoed nudes at a villa in the town of Arcetri was probably an isolated act of scruple on the part of the family in residence. In fact the Church remained the chief patron of sculptors and painters throughout the Renaissance.

Neither did church doctrine, with its laws against such things as the taking of interest on a loan, affect the progress of economic life toward capitalism. Either by subterfuge, or quite openly—depending on his own conscience or the attitude of the local bishop—the Renaissance banker and merchant made his pile without feeling that he was cutting himself off from his church. He kept a conscience-account, *il conto di Messer Domeneddio,* for contributions to charity in the same spirit that his present-day successors give large sums for philanthropic purposes.

There were humanists, like Pico della Mirandola, who were particularly concerned with spiritual matters. Though they drew upon spiritual streams far from Christian theology, they were interested in demonstrating that all civilizations and all philosophy had been irradiated by the Christian God—some consciously, and some unconsciously—before the revelation of the birth of Christ. It is true that humanism did pave the way for the Reformation, did help divide Christendom into two. But it did not do it intentionally. The humanist practice of tracing ideas back to their source in classical literature destroyed much of the authority of medieval documents—including the theological treatises of medieval monks. Thus the claim of Rome to be the interpreter of Christian doctrine, as well as Christ's representative on earth, was thrown open to question. Then, too, humanist thought, with its element of mysticism, especially in the writings of the Neoplatonists, prepared men for the idea of direct communication with God—an idea that was one of the cornerstones of Protestantism. But neither of these two trends in humanism was recognized as a serious threat by Renaissance ecclesiastics.

What did seem a threat to them was humanism's concentration on ethics, its attempt to show that the good life could be lived on ethical terms, on a man's relations with other men, rather than his relations with God. Some humanists tended to put Christ in a pantheon, among other wise men; some were dubious about the survival of a personal soul, as opposed to a generalized human soul; some believed that a man's fate was governed less by the will of God than by the orderly planets and constellations which patrolled His heavens. They never saw themselves as opponents of orthodox religion, but they did emphasize the importance of learning how to live rather than how to die. When the Church's Fifth Lateran council, in 1513, condemned doubts about personal immortality and reliance on heathen philosophers, it was trying to stanch that unstemmable stream of thought that flowed from Renaissance humanism into the 20th Century.

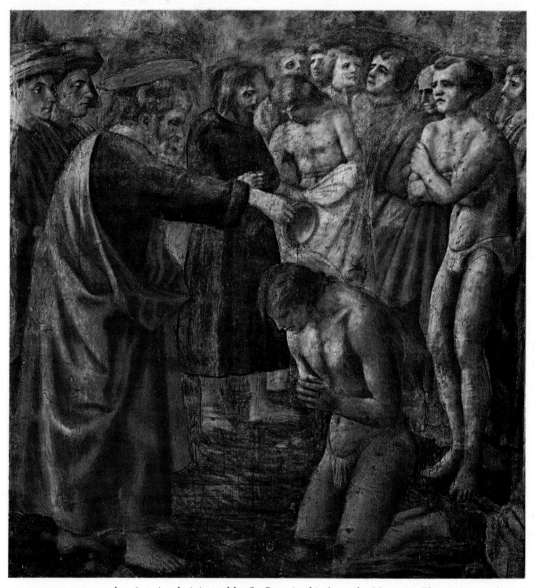

THE FIRST SACRAMENT, *baptism, is administered by St. Peter in this fresco by Masaccio. The sacraments bound all men—the fervent reformers and purists along with the worldly priests and popes—to a common faith.*

THE FERMENT OF FAITH

The Renaissance Church was concerned with man's life in this world as much as the next. Its servants were everywhere—staffing hospitals; teaching in schools; running loan offices, orphan asylums and almshouses. Some of the clergy, semi-literate parish priests and greedy bishops, tarnished the image of their Church. At the same time, there were large numbers of wandering friars and reform-minded preachers whose fiery sermons stirred whole cities to renewed faith. If popes were often politicians who used Church offices as patronage, they did so in defense of a papal state at war with its neighbors. In an age of great ferment, a worldly spirit and a vitality of faith were essential ingredients of the Church.

64   A HOUSEHOLD SHRINE *of the 15th Century, with a simple terra-cotta sculpture of the Virgin and Child, is still used by humble worshipers in Florence.*

SPLENDORS AND SIMPLE SHRINES

In an Italian city of the Renaissance, it was never far to a place of worship. Shrines were everywhere, on street corners and in courtyards—wherever people were wont to pass. In these shrines, a worshiper left a candle, or some flowers, and asked a favor of the Virgin. Increasingly, Mary was depicted as a humble woman, far more human than the gilded Madonnas of medieval art.

Every city had its magnificent cathedral, too—a showpiece of worldly splendor encrusted with fine paintings and sculpture. Built by city governments, princes and popes, they reflected the earthly power of the Church and its patrons. The churches erected by Cosimo de' Medici, wrote a 16th Century biographer, "were intended to be permanent and always witness to his fame." When services were held in these cathedrals, the seats were reserved for the rich; the poor were required to stand at the rear.

WORK-WORN HANDS *identify this serene Madonna with the poor. In this work by the Sicilian Antonello da Messina, the Virgin is seen as Holy Mother, instead of the exalted Queen of Heaven.*

RADIANT FIGURES *of the Queen of Sheba and Constantine the Great decorate a church at Arezzo. The paintings by Piero della Francesca reflect the pomp and power of the Church.*

A PANELED PULPIT, *sculptured by Donatello in the Tuscan town of Prato, enabled preachers to address great throngs out of doors.*

THE FIERY PREACHERS
OF REPENTANCE

For all its worldliness, 15th Century Italy was constantly being called upon to repent. In Siena a hermit sent a child through the streets bearing a skull on a stick, warning of damnation. In Milan another prophet seized the pulpit of the great cathedral and from it delivered sermons of doom for many months. Everywhere wandering Preachers of Repentance drew great crowds to hear them denounce the abuses of the clergy and the pope, often speaking from outdoor pulpits or courtyards. After a sermon, there would commonly be a "bonfire of vanities," as the aroused populace burned their worldly books, paintings and false hairpieces.

AROUSING THE FAITHFUL, *St. Vincent Ferrer, a Preacher of Repentance,*

delivers a sermon in the courtyard of a Verona church. Drawing crowds wherever he went, he led great revivals in France, Flanders and Spain.

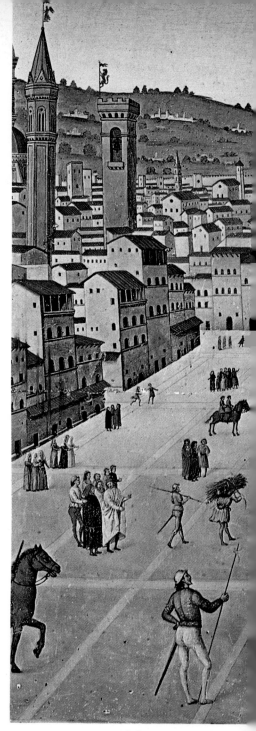

A FIERY DEATH is provided for Savonarola outside the town hall of Florence, as portrayed in this 15th Century painting. Of the small band of the friar's followers in the square, only a few dare to look at the pyre.

A FOLLOWER'S GRIEF is evoked in this painting by Botticelli. The artist was himself converted by Savonarola, whose sermons were so moving that his disciples were popularly referred to as the "Piagnoni," the Weepers.

SAVONAROLA - THE SCOURGE OF FLORENCE

The Preachers of Repentance were frequently critics of the political, as well as the spiritual, order. In Florence, the Dominican friar Savonarola denounced Lorenzo de' Medici as a tyrant. After the Florentines deposed the governing Medicis and turned to Savonarola, he virtually ruled the city from a monastery. But his zeal for reform made powerful enemies. Finally, his tirades against the Pope led to his excommunication and arrest—a fatal blow to him and to his movement. He was burned at the stake, and only a few of his followers were bold enough to gather around him at the end.

AN AUSTERE CELL *in San Marco (left) is decorated with one of Fra Angelico's frescoes, portraying the Crucifixion. It was said that Fra Angelico never painted without first praying, and wept whenever he painted Christ.*

THE QUIET FAITH OF THE FRIARS

While many monks of the time were ministering to the world, others retired to monasteries. Upholding the precept of St. Jerome that a monk ought to mourn rather than teach, some monasteries retained elements of religious fervor. In the monastery of San Marco in Florence, from which Savonarola crusaded against the "ribald Church," a Dominican monk named Fra Angelico depicted the abiding faith of the friars in scores of frescoes. He filled his paintings with serene saints and simple monks *(opposite)*—although in one fresco he could not resist showing monks of the rival Franciscan order roasting in Hell. As Fra Angelico's fame spread, the Pope offered to make him Archbishop of Florence. The artist declined—preferring the monk's simple cowl to the Archbishop's miter.

A MONUMENT OF FAITH

The magnificent St. Peter's basilica *(above)*, built to replace a 1200-year-old church that stood over St. Peter's grave, was the final great statement of the faith and the worldliness embodied in the Renaissance Church. The popes of the age were avid patrons of the arts—and the Renaissance artists did much of their greatest work in the service of the Church.

St. Peter's basilica was their most ambitious collaboration.
The work was begun in 1506, after several architects had submitted rival plans to Pope Julius II. Donato Bramante's winning design aroused stormy opposition—as did the taxes which Julius and later popes levied in order to pay for the work. Soon great masters like Raphael and Michelangelo, and a succession of lesser artists, were making repeated and often drastic changes. When the Cathedral was finished in 1626, only the great dome—which Michelangelo designed— bore a resemblance to the original plan. Overlooking the piazza stand huge, baroque statues of the saints on a colonnade of pillars, both designed decades later by Lorenzo Bernini.

4

FLORENCE:
INTELLECTUAL DYNAMO

Despite the wealth of Venice and the power of Rome, to think of Renaissance Italy is to think, first and foremost, of Florence, the city that led all other Italian cities in both daring and achievement. Florence not only produced a series of great men; it supported an atmosphere of inquiry and experiment that made it a great laboratory. It was the testing ground for most of the Renaissance's political and artistic ideas. From the early 14th to the mid-16th Century no other city in Italy, indeed in Europe, kept up such a steady pressure of intellectual attainment. Look for a moment at the roll call of great names of the Italian Renaissance: In poetry, Dante and Poliziano; in prose, Boccaccio and Machiavelli; in painting, Giotto, Masaccio, Uccello, Verrocchio, Fra Angelico, Fra Filippo Lippi, Botticelli, Leonardo da Vinci, Pontormo; in sculpture, Donatello, Luca della Robbia, Ghiberti, Michelangelo, Cellini; in architecture, Brunelleschi, Leon Battista Alberti, Michelozzo, the Sangallo brothers. All were Florentines. In philosophy the most memorable name is that of Marsilio Ficino; in the writing of history, the names of Leonardo Bruni, Guicciardini, Jacopo Nardi. All are Florentine names. The best-known banks in Europe in the 14th Century were those of the Bardi and the Peruzzi; in the 15th Century, that of the Medici. All of these were Florentine banks. In fact one Florentine family, more than any other, is identified with both the culture and the politics of the Renaissance: the family of the Medici.

True, Florence was not always the pioneer. The foundations of modern business methods were laid in 13th Century Genoa. Humanism was born in Verona and Padua at the turn of the 13th Century. Pisa gave her name to two trail blazers of Renaissance sculpture, the father and son Nicola and Giovanni Pisano. The techniques of modern diplomacy were worked out first of all by Venetian trading consuls. But what Florence did not originate, it refined. Many of the greatest non-Florentine artists came, like Piero della Francesca and Raphael, to "dip their clothes in the Arno" and had their styles crucially changed there. And Savonarola, a friar from Ferrara, reached his height as a perfervid preacher in the environment of what he called "the cleverest people in Italy."

MASKED SINGERS, *led by Lorenzo de' Medici (at left), serenade the women of Florence during the spring carnival season. Lorenzo often wrote bawdy carnival songs for such diverse groups as shoemakers, bakers and even beggars.*

PHYSICIANS AND APOTHECARIES   MASONS AND CARPENTERS

What made it possible for Florence to set the tone for almost every aspect of Renaissance life? The answer is much easier to describe than explain. Genius cannot be accounted for; the best we can do is to examine the atmosphere that encourages it to flourish.

Geography comes first. No great city has ever been built far from the water—either ocean or river —and the fortunes of Florence began when the Etruscan hill town of Fiesole was refounded by the Romans on the flat land beside the River Arno. The city was now more vulnerable, but it had easy access to an important trade route. It had good communications by river to the west, and practicable passes through the mountains in other directions. And, as the extension of the city's boundaries show, Florence quietly boomed.

Florentia, as the Roman town was called, was a rectangle enclosed by streets that are still there: Via Tornabuoni, Via de' Cerretani, Via del Proconsolo, Via Porta Rossa. The grid of streets has a military regularity which marks it off from the erratic sprawl that characterized the city's medieval expansion. Except for these, nothing of the old Roman town is left. There was, however, a Roman amphitheater which stood outside the town's eastern walls; the curve of the present-day Via Torta and Via dei Bentaccordi define it. And Via delle Terme records the site of the baths which stood outside the walls on the south.

At some time in the Dark Ages, as though reach-

ing toward the commercial importance that still lay in the future, the town extended its southern limit past the Roman baths in a triangle that reached further toward the river. By 1172 the suburbs had increased to such an extent that it was decided to enclose them in another circuit of walls. North of the Arno this new wall ran in a square, with its base on the river. It can still be traced by going up Via de' Benci in the east, turning left at Via Sant' Egidio, and back to Piazza Goldoni down Via del Giglio. Via de' Fossi, just before Piazza Goldoni, is named for the ditches that fronted this second circuit of walls. Florence now straddled the Arno, enclosing a shallow arc of the Oltr' Arno, the district south of the river.

As traffic rose between the north and south banks, three bridges were added to the original one, the Ponte Vecchio, which dated back to Roman times but had been rebuilt after its collapse in 1178. By this time Florence had about 30,000 inhabitants. And still it grew. Suburbs once more sprang up outside the walls and in 1284 a third and vaster barricade was begun, catching the two preceding ones behind its armor. Its line, a rough semicircle, can be followed along the great boulevards built in the 19th Century from Piazza Beccaria to Piazza della Libertà and down to Piazza Vittorio Veneto. Long sections of this 13th Century wall can still be seen south of the river; it climbs up Via di Belvedere, runs along the top of the Boboli Gardens, descends to meet the river beyond

the Porta San Frediano. Soon after it was finished, in 1328, the city's population had risen to 120,000, and if the wave of plagues that began with the Black Death in 1348 had not reduced this population by about one half, still another circuit of walls might have become necessary. As it was, when this third circuit was inspected in 1526, during a period of almost constant warfare, there were houses stretching far beyond it into the country. The Florentine government had them pulled down, to provide a clear field for cannon fire from the walls.

Florence, by the time of the Renaissance, was large, rich, and by the standards of those days, stable. The organs of government somehow kept functioning, even if from time to time they were emptied of one faction and filled with the supporters of another. The city's street names are reminders: Via della Condotta (behind the Palazzo Ugoccioni) is named for the government committee that paid the republic's soldiers; Vicolo dell'Onestà (near the Via dei Speziali) for the magistrates in charge of public decency who licensed Renaissance prostitutes; Piazza della Signoria for the Signoria (or priorate), the chief executive officers of state, who continued to guide the city's political and economic fortunes no matter how rapidly they went in and out of office.

Significantly, too, one of the most familiar groups of street names records the Renaissance city's thriving day-to-day commercial life. Via dei Saponai is named for the soap makers; Via dei Speziali for the druggists; Via dell'Ariento for the silversmiths. And Via delle Belle Donne—street of the lovely ladies—may or may not commemorate the oldest trade of all.

The street names are also reminders of the 15th Century's conspiracies and assassinations. Borgo degli Albizzi is named for the family who were the chief rivals of the Medici. In 1433, Rinaldo degli Albizzi had Cosimo de' Medici banished from Florence; a year later Cosimo returned and it was Rinaldo's turn to be banished. Piazza dei Pazzi (behind the Palazzo Pazzi) memorializes the Pazzi family, who plotted to kill Lorenzo de' Medici at High Mass in the Cathedral of Santa Maria del Fiore, in 1478. Lorenzo fought his way to safety in the sacristy, but his brother Giuliano was stabbed to death, suffering 19 dagger wounds.

It was a city of crimes, violence and revolutions. But there was also a fundamental continuity to Florentine life that enabled men to go about their business with reasonable confidence. The republic increased its territories and grew in prestige and self-esteem—the latter was a quality the Florentines possessed in abundant measure. This continuity, especially of republican forms of government, gives the lie to the view that the great cultural flowering of the Renaissance sprang from the tingling excitement of living in violent and insecure times. There was another influence, equally strong, which may also have helped to produce an atmosphere in which culture could flourish. This was the existence, in Florence, of a kaleidoscopic society made up of many social and economic parts, each group wanting works of art and literature to suit its own tastes, and all of them sharing a civic pride based on the assumption that all literate men shared in forming the city's destiny.

If there was any one industry in Florence which tended to divide the merchants and the proletariat,

SHIPS *carried raw wool from England and Spain to Italy. In Florence, a city as well known for its weavers as for its artists, the wool industry set thousands to work, in the efficient production process detailed here.*

SORTING, *a team of graders separated the wool into three groups of fine, medium and coarse strands. Sorting was only one of some 30 separate steps in processing wool; each step involved a large team of specialized workers.*

DYEING *was done after the wool had been beaten, cleaned and soaked in oil (cheap wools were dyed later, after weaving). Florentine cloth was prized in Europe, Persia— even in China—mainly for its brilliant colors.*

it was the wool business, which together with banking was the basis of Florentine wealth. The Florentine merchant class was a large one, and comprised many income groups. Its membership was fluid, and its edges blurred—for several reasons. Fluctuations in the wool trade and a continuous influx of new families from the countryside kept the economic ladder a busy thoroughfare of comings and goings. Personal fortunes prospered and waned. Then, too, marriage partnerships and business alliances gave most merchant families connections at different income levels.

There were, by the time of the Renaissance, 21 important guilds, all of which had grown from voluntary associations of men with common business interests to large corporations. Especially was this true of the seven great guilds, whose members were the city's richest and most influential businessmen—the judges and notaries; cloth importers and refinishers; cloth manufacturers; leading retailers and silk merchants; moneychangers; furriers; and physicians and apothecaries. But the 14 lesser guilds were also something of a force, politically, if not financially. They were articulate and well organized, and their members—artisans and shopkeepers—stabilized Florentine commercial life. These lesser guilds, usually called the craft guilds, included butchers; shoemakers; blacksmiths; builders; secondhand dealers; wine-dealers; innkeepers; sellers of salt, oil and cheese; tanners; armorers;

ironworkers; girdlemakers; woodworkers; bakers.

Between the two groups of guilds—rich merchants and craftsmen—there was a sort of grudging respect; neither could disregard the other. And although Florence was under the control of the rich merchants throughout most of her life as a republic, internal convulsions and political compromise did give the poorer man an occasional voice in city affairs. The result of this was to preserve Florence's turbulent republicanism far longer than was possible among most of the other Italian states, which fell early and permanently into despotism.

Florence's mercantile republic also had little to fear from the extremes of its population—the nobility and the proletariat. There was no direct conflict of interest between merchant and lord, between industrial-based and agrarian-based wealth. The late-13th Century Ordinances of Justice had debarred the nobility from high government office, but the lords had contracted family and business links with members of the greater guilds which gave them considerable influence on civic affairs. And with nobles entering business (like merchants) and merchants investing in land in the country (like nobles), there was a mutual interest based on common concerns. Thus, although the noble element certainly complicated the rivalry between families of the *popolo grasso*, there was no danger that the nobles as a class could take over power. Similarly the merchants did not worry unduly about the

COMBING *the wool separated the long strands from the short tufts of fuzz. Then the long strands, wound on wooden blocks, went directly to the spinners. The tufts were used too, but first had to be prepared by carders.*

CARDING *was a scraping process applied to lower-grade wool. Spreading the wool on wicker frames, workers untangled it with wire scrapers—tools so efficient Florence forbade anyone to take them out of the city.*

SPINNING *was usually done in the country, where peasant women worked in their own homes, converting wool into yarn. They were constantly busy, since at its height Florence produced some 80,000 bolts of wool a year.*

lower classes. Although the Florentine proletariat was large, exploited and bitterly dissatisfied, it only revolted successfully once, in 1378. The Ciompi uprising, as it was called, was an attempt by the woolworkers to get a voice in the city government. Although their revolt failed after a few weeks, largely because of a lack of leadership, nonetheless some concessions were made and, for the first time in Florentine history, the lowest class was represented. But even this political innovation lasted less than four years. It was put down by the whole employer class in panic-stricken reaction, and the proletarian guilds were forever dissolved.

Florence's experience with despotism—unlike that of Italy generally—was also brief. There were three episodes of dictatorship, in 1313-1322, in 1325-1330 and in 1342-1343. Each one involved a foreigner, called in time of crisis to deal with a political or military emergency. And each one was thrown out by a wave of general revulsion that swung the pendulum back to republicanism. Thereafter, except in one instance, Florence remained under the control of the upper-class merchants. The one case in which it did not followed the despotism of Walter of Brienne, a French soldier of fortune who had been called in in 1342 to resolve one of the city's periodic military crises. Brienne's invitation came from certain elements in the upper classes, and he was given lifelong despotic powers. However, he quickly antagonized his rich supporters over a mat-

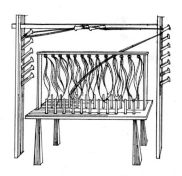

WARPING *was the process of looping strands of wool (center) over the pegs of a frame, preparatory to weaving. Workers stretched the wool on this frame and stiffened it with a gum. It was now ready for the loom.*

WEAVING *was the last step, transforming yarn into cloth that Florentine merchants would sell to the world. A handful of wealthy merchants ran the whole industry, whose peak employment was some 30,000 workers.*

ter of taxes. Soon he had succeeded in so outraging all elements of Florentine society that they got together and expelled him after only a year's rule. In the aftermath of his expulsion the *popolo grasso* was prevented from reassuming power and the *popolo minuto* took over the majority of government offices for the next 40 years. Then, however, after the Ciompi uprising, the *popolo grasso* once again reasserted their power.

From its successful weathering of crises—political, military, economic—Florence came to believe that its form of government represented all that was finest in Italy's tradition. This belief crystallized into an idea when, at the turn of the 14th Century, the republic triumphed over the efforts of the Milanese despot to terrify it into surrender. Thereafter, and throughout most of the 15th Century, this idealization of the republic was so potent that few of the Florentines realized that only the façade of republicanism was being preserved. It was not until shortly before the death of Lorenzo de' Medici that Florence suddenly woke up to the fact that the state, for all its republican forms, had drifted into the control of one family. Then, after Lorenzo's death in 1492 and a brief but disastrous period of control by his arrogant son, the city—as if to rid itself of a charming dream—expelled the Medici and redrafted its constitution, giving it a much broader democratic base. Thus, for most of the Renaissance, Florence either was, or believed itself to be, a government of the people.

In a commercial city economic and political life cannot be separated; political figures are business figures. In Florence, the political prestige of the Medici family was bolstered by the international fame of their bank, and the economic strength of the guilds inevitably played a part in politics. The city's atmosphere was the atmosphere of commerce: pragmatic and competitive. In spite of the crash of personal fortunes and the shared hard-ships of depressions, Florence's spirit was hopeful. It met the challenge of bad times by improving its business techniques and industrial organization, so as to cut corners and lower costs. The Florentines believed in human ingenuity. Only when faced by forces beyond their control, like drought or continual rain, did they turn to miracle-working devices for help. There is a superb palace in the Piazza Santa Trinità that is a monument to this spirit of enterprise. It was built just before 1520 by the youngest of three brothers, Bartolini Salimbene. According to legend news came to the brothers one morning that one of their ships had docked in Pisa with a rich freight from the east. To sell the cargo, it was necessary to fix prices—but the elder brothers would not forgo their midday siesta. Bartolini, however, galloped to Pisa and bargained himself into a fortune—with which he built his palace. Over the window pediments he carved the motto *Per non dormire:* "It does not pay to sleep."

Wakefulness paid off for many Florentine businessmen, none more handsomely than the Medici bankers. Their bank, while not so large as the 14th Century banks of the Peruzzi and Bardi families, was politically the most important in all of Florentine history. Its connections outside Florence, particularly with the French court and the papacy, influenced Florence's outside political alignments. And within the city it became so powerful politically that Lorenzo de' Medici on at least one occasion could, with impunity, dip into public funds to restore its credit. The bank was founded in 1397 by Giovanni di Bicci de' Medici and steadily expanded up to the death of Cosimo de' Medici in 1464. By Cosimo's time it had branches in Rome, Venice, Milan and Pisa, as well as Florence. Outside Italy there were branches in Geneva, Lyons, Avignon, Bruges and London. Each branch was a self-contained unit, dealing with other branches exactly as it did with customers. Thus, the branch managers were free to make decisions on their own, and to take advantage of local fluctuations in prices and the value of money. But the arrangement meant that control from the parent bank was weak, and that the bank's fortunes as a whole depended largely on a wise choice of managers.

Like modern banks, its activities were varied. Most of the profits came from conventional banking services; it accepted deposits from its customers, made transfers for them, extended loans and collected revenues. But since a number of its customers were institutions—most notably, the Medici were bankers to the Church—the extent of these activities was wide indeed. In addition the Medici branches dabbled in trade, buying and selling wool, cloth, oil, spices and citrus fruit on their own, and sometimes entering into temporary partnership with other merchants. Through such arrangements they bought brocades, jewels and silver plate for their aristocratic clients. At one time their investments even blossomed into a virtual monopoly of the mining and sale of an essential ingredient in the textile industry: alum. This chemical was used to clean the fiber and fix the dye in woolen cloth.

Before 1462 most of Europe's best-quality alum had come from Asia Minor but in that year deposits at Tolfa in the Papal States were recognized as an acceptable substitute and in 1466 the Medici bank was called in to manage them. Pope Paul II helped his bankers to help themselves by forbidding Christians to import alum from Moslem countries. And when a smaller rival deposit in Ischia threatened to provide a possible Christian competitor, the Medici hastily concluded a cartel agreement with its proprietor to preserve their monopoly by establishing a quota system which limited both Ischian and Tolfan production. Big business took a further step toward modernity when discovery of yet another deposit near Volterra, in Tuscany itself, prompted Lorenzo de' Medici to force through

a claim to exploit it. When the citizens, fired by this as well as by other grievances, revolted from Florentine rule, the rising was crushed and the city sacked. Ironically, Volterra's alum deposit proved to be a small one, never commercially successful.

This vigorous pursuit of alum holdings was not, however, typical of the bank's conduct under Lorenzo. After the death of Cosimo its fortunes declined, and by 1494 it was in virtual bankruptcy. In part this was due to external forces—the taking over of interests in the Levant by the Turks and a trade recession that brought bank after bank to its knees all over Europe. But part of the responsibility for the Medici bankruptcy was Lorenzo's. He had not received the stern business education that was needed for survival in an age where profit was increasingly hard to come by; his tastes were those of a statesman and a dilettante rather than those of a banker. Furthermore he lacked Cosimo's flair for making shrewd appointments to branch offices. Staffed by hesitant men who needed but did not get forceful guidance from above, the bank capitulated to circumstances. *Per non dormire* can stand as a motto for Lorenzo's attitude to politics, love and the arts, but not to banking.

It is hazardous to say what direct influence the Florentine political atmosphere had upon the city's culture, but it seems more than pure coincidence that there are parallels between the two:

¶ Florence was expedient about government; it looked at political situations realistically and developed solutions for them. It also pioneered in realism in the arts.

¶ It saw itself as following in the political spirit of republican Rome—and it followed the theories and practices of ancient Roman art.

¶ It was enormously conscious of its political dignity and destiny. At the same time it produced a literature laden with self-eulogy, and the funds for many of its buildings and works of art were raised by appealing to the people's desire to enhance the city's beauty and fame.

¶ Its citizens were intensely interested in political developments—and got involved in passionate discussions over the commissioning of public art.

But if art and politics can be linked only circumstantially, there is no such problem with art and commerce. The influence of Florentine merchants on culture was direct: they bought it. They bought it in prosperity to salve their consciences and in adversity as a consolation and an investment. To be very rich in republican Florence was to run two risks. Affluence aroused the jealousy of other citizens, and also their suspicions—too much money earned in banking made it clear that the Church's injunction against taking interest had been flouted on a large scale. The religious censure could be bought off by building and decorating churches, the jealousy assuaged by liberal spending that purported to be for the greater glory of the state. In a note to his children Lorenzo de' Medici wrote: "I find we have spent a large sum of money from 1434 up to 1471, as appears from an account book covering that period. It shows an incredible sum, for it amounts to 663,755 florins spent on buildings, charities and taxes, not counting other expenses; nor would I complain about this, for though many a man would like to have even part of that sum in his purse I think it gave great luster to the state and this money seems to be well spent."

The sum, mainly spent in Cosimo's time, was a formidable one: a painter with the reputation of Botticelli would have gotten between 50 and 100 florins for a picture. That Cosimo's account book lumps buildings and charities together supports the remark by his contemporary biographer, Vespasiano da Bisticci, who wrote that Cosimo had "prickings of conscience that certain portions of his wealth had not been righteously gained," and

that his prolific church-building was an act of penance. But it was also an act of pride. Through their dealings with the aristocratic French courts in the north, the Medici and other wealthy bankers and merchants had acquired a taste for pomp and display. In bourgeois Florence, however, they had to be cautious. The Medici rejected plans for a sumptuous palace and commissioned a far less ostentatious one, now the Palazzo Medici-Riccardi. But on hallowed ground a certain flaunting of wealth and influence seemed reasonably safe; the Medici arms appear on all the churches that Cosimo built. His son Piero, however, displayed a little more delicacy. Realizing that the family arms—the six red balls—might well be offensive to others, he limited himself to a display of his personal arms only when he paid for a tabernacle in San Miniato. But Piero's restraint could not last. The opportunity offered by a marble temple built by him for one of the holiest objects in Florence—the miraculous painting of the Annunciation in the church of Santissima Annunziata—was too much for him. On it he had carved *Costò fior. 4 mila el marmo solo:* "the marble alone cost 4,000 florins."

Since churches were safe outlets for display, wealth fostered the art objects most appropriate to them—paintings, sculptures, painted glass—rather than objects for domestic consumption. And since paintings and sculpture were thus open to public praise and criticism, a healthy rivalry grew up among artists. But Florentine painters and sculptors were also stimulated by their patrons. Through their humanist education and their continued interest in humanist learning, these wealthy Florentines developed a lively interest in the process of creation, as well as the finished work of art. They wished increasingly to be judged for their taste as well as their munificence, and this led them to encourage artists like Botticelli to work in "advanced" and idiosyncratic styles.

The influence of those top-drawer taste-makers was widely felt. For one thing, it was copied by some of their lesser business associates. Francesco Sassetti and Giovanni Tornabuoni were Medici managers, and though otherwise not especially interested in the intellectual movements of the day, they both commissioned Ghirlandaio to paint frescoes. Sassetti's was in the family chapel in Santa Trinità, and Tornabuoni's was in the chancel of Santa Maria Novella.

At a still lower level of penetration, rich merchants influenced the selection of works of art commissioned by guilds or civic groups which were uncertain of their own judgment. The statue of St. George by Donatello probably represents, in its refinement, the tastes of only a small minority of the weaponmakers whose guild paid for it. The guild sought advice among those who were more knowledgeable. Without the existence of this Florentine wealthy educated class the impulse of artists themselves to evolve from medieval styles might have been far weaker.

The taste of the rich, then, set the tone for art. But the mercantile atmosphere of Florence as a whole may also have provided encouragement. Art follows its own inner laws of growth and the special talents of individual artists, but it can also be affected by the tempo of a society. Working in the midst of financial realists, the Florentine artist may have been stimulated to move toward realism faster than he would have elsewhere. The average Florentine businessman knew what things were for and what they cost—houses, fields, vineyards. The thought of profit was close to the surface of his mind. This consciousness of real value, as opposed to symbolic value, carried over into other areas of his life. He was aware of his own worth as a person. Other men might do great deeds on the battlefield for which they would be remembered by poets and chroniclers, but he, too, was a

LEADING A GIRAFFE, *an emissary of the Egyptian Sultan is portrayed bringing the beast as a gift to Lorenzo de' Medici. Lorenzo donated the giraffe to Florence's famed menagerie, where, only two blocks from the Palazzo Vecchio, Florentines could also see caged bears, an elephant or a den of lions.*

man of accomplishments: he had made money, paid his taxes, kept careful accounts. He wanted to be remembered by posterity. So he had himself painted into the pictures he ordered for his church —a supplicant kneeling in a corner, a bystander in a crowd. And since there is no point in being painted unless you can be recognized, he asked to be painted as he was: it is no coincidence that Florence was first to stress realistic portraiture.

These merchantlike qualities did not actually bring about Giotto's unique way of recording the world, or the style of Masaccio, but they almost certainly sustained them and helped them to have followers. The tendency in Florentine painting for much of the 14th and 15th Centuries was in the direction of a precise rendering of external reality. It may have been an art directed, as one Florentine writer scornfully remarked, toward men who "say it is enough to be able to sign your own name and be able to strike the balance in a ledger." But without this basis of mastered realism the work of the giants of the late Renaissance could never have been so intensely personal. Raphael, Michelangelo and Titian took the efficient recording of men and nature for granted, and went on from there to imbue reality with their own private vision.

The arts also flourished in Florence through their use as propaganda. The fact that Giotto was employed in other cities—Padua, Assisi, Naples— was a source of pride to later Florentines, and by the time of Lorenzo de' Medici, artists were being used rather like cultural ambassadors. Lorenzo recommended his favorite architect, Giuliano da Sangallo, to the King of Naples, and proposed the painters Ghirlandaio and Botticelli to Pope Sixtus IV as fresco painters for the Sistine Chapel. And he almost certainly supported Leonardo's application to work for Lodovico Sforza in Milan.

Florence even put up monuments to its famous painters: to Filippo Lippi in the cathedral at Spoleto, where he died; to Giotto in the cathedral in Florence, with inscriptions composed by Lorenzo's own chief literary adviser, Angelo Poliziano. And in no other city were artists made more aware of the important role they played in the city's life. Time after time there are triumphant references in Florentine literature to the city's primacy in the arts. In 1436 the architect-painter-writer Leon Battista Alberti wrote the first treatise on the theory of painting. In his prologue, addressed to the painter-sculptor-architect Brunelleschi, he said: "When I compared the arts and letters of the ancients with those of modern times, I thought that nature, mistress of those arts, had grown worn out, and no longer produced the mighty and well contrived works with which, in her glorious youth, she had been so lavish. But since I have returned to this country of ours from the long exile . . . I have perceived in many—first in you, Filippo, and then in our dear friend Donato [Donatello], and in those others, Nenci [Ghiberti], Luca [Luca della Robbia] and Masaccio, a talent for all praiseworthy arts which the most famous of ancient cities did not excel."

To give but one example of the buoyant confidence which this sort of treatment must have instilled in artists, the goldsmith Bernardo Cennini, without regular training as a printer, designed, cut and cast the type of a superb edition of a commentary on Vergil, announcing at the end of the book: *Florentinis ingeniis nihil ardui est—* "nothing is beyond the powers of the Florentines." His sentiments were echoed by all of Florence. Patriotic, educated in the classics but disciplined by the expediencies of business and politics, the city recognized the role of the individual. By adding an informed self-consciousness to genius of every type, Florence gave genius a sense of direction that led from the Middle Ages to the modern world.

LUCREZIA BORGIA

CESARE BORGIA

ISABELLA D'ESTE

LORENZO DE' MEDICI

ANDREAS VESALIUS

ANDREA MANTEGNA

ALDUS MANUTIUS

THE QUEST FOR FAME

Renaissance Italy was a place in which men from all ranks of life dreamed of fame
—and often won it, by fair means or foul. In "the desire to perpetuate a name,"
said Machiavelli, those "who could distinguish themselves by nothing praiseworthy, strove to do so by infamous deeds." In 1537, for example, an obscure
cousin of Lorenzo de' Medici murdered a Florentine duke, simply to immortalize
his own name. It was an age of flamboyant figures, seven of whom are shown
above. Each was a virtuoso—a word that came into the Italian language during the
Renaissance to describe the towering personality who made an art of his every act.

THE STUDY OF A WOMAN OF WIT

Isabella d'Este, whose apartment is shown opposite, was the most brilliant woman of her age, related by birth or marriage to almost every ruler in Italy. When her husband, the Marquis of Mantua, was captured in a war with Venice, Isabella ruled Mantua by her wit—even disarming enemies her husband had previously made. Returning at last from Venice, the Marquis complained, "It is our fate to have as a wife a woman who is always ruled by her head." She was, said a poet, "the prima donna of the world." At 60, when she sat for a portrait by the great Titian, she thought it so unflattering that she ordered him to do another —showing her as she had looked 40 years earlier.

A COURTLY CORRESPONDENCE *kept Isabella in touch with all events in Italy. Her quill rests on a letter to her husband; beside it is a polite note from Cesare Borgia, Duke of Romagna, asking her to send some more of her excellent hunting dogs.*

A SUMPTUOUS RETREAT, *Isabella d'Este's study in the ducal palace of Mantua contained so many costly books and great art works that it was called "il Paradiso." The ceiling is carved with her name and realistic motto, "Neither hope nor fear."*

THE MEDICI VILLA *outside Florence was frequented by the city's most famous artists, writers and musicians. The gardens, laid out in ancient Roman*

A BANK LEDGER *shows the accounts of the Milan branch of the Medici bank. The bank, which dominated European finance for a century, had branches in 10 cities throughout the Continent.*

HOME HAUNTS OF "THE MAGNIFICENT"

Lorenzo de' Medici, known throughout Italy as "The Magnificent," seemed to lead a dozen lives at once. A Florentine prince, he was engaged in endless negotiations with neighboring states, maintaining a precarious peace. His villa, at left, was a gathering place for the greatest men of the age. As head of the Medici bank, he masterminded extensive financial deals—transactions so large and so tricky that they ultimately contributed to the bank's collapse. His versatility and daring won him great renown. When war broke out with Naples, Lorenzo sailed to the Neapolitan court, appearing unarmed and alone—and persuaded the king to withdraw his troops from Tuscany. One pope excommunicated him—yet he so completely won over the next that an envoy to the Vatican commented: "The Pope slept with the eyes of Lorenzo the Magnificent."

fashion, were planted with cypress and myrtle, the trees of antiquity.

THE BIRTHPLACE
OF MODERN MEDICINE

A surgeon, teacher and brilliant anatomist, Andreas Vesalius was the founder of modern medicine. Before his time, Renaissance doctors still slavishly followed the precepts of the ancient Greeks, relying chiefly on the works of Galen, a Greek physician of the Second Century A.D. who had based many of his conclusions about human anatomy on dissections of Barbary apes. As a student Vesalius developed his own ideas about anatomy, performing dozens of dissections and collecting bones to study from graveyards, public gallows and mortuaries. At the University of Padua he was so outstanding a student that he won his degree in medicine at the age of 23—and a day later the university appointed him Professor of Surgery. The amphitheater where he lectured and dissected was always packed with students and colleagues. Still in his twenties, he published his findings in a voluminous treatise, *The Fabric of the Human Body*, illustrated with more than 270 detailed woodcuts. The book made many new contentions—for example, that the gall bladder did not open into the stomach; that there was no bone in the heart. Some doctors were outraged, but within a year Vesalius had been so thoroughly vindicated that he was booked for lectures at three universities. At the University of Pisa the crowds struggled so hard to get a better view of Vesalius at his dissecting table that the entire operating theater, built for the occasion, collapsed.

A MEDICAL HANDBOOK, *this 1491 text, used by Vesalius, lies on a balustrade at Padua beside a Renaissance cap and gown. Padua's medical school was so famous that the sick came from all over Europe to be treated.*

THE LECTURE HALL *at Padua is the oldest medical amphitheater in existence. Here Vesalius' work was carried forward; on the table are early medical texts and dissecting tools.*

THE BORGIAS' INFAMOUS DOMAIN

The notorious Borgias were envied for their elegant castles and feared for their dismal dungeons. The father, Rodrigo, used every form of skulduggery to gain the papal throne. As Pope Alexander VI he and his son Cesare used the papal armies to depose a host of petty despots. Lucrezia was married off to three rulers before she was 22; her father, as Pope, annulled the first marriage, and Cesare ended the second by having the groom murdered. But the family fortunes suddenly plunged. Alexander was fatally stricken with malaria. Soon after, Cesare died in battle. Distraught, Lucrezia donned a hair shirt and engaged in extensive charities—even pawning her jewels in order to give alms.

A DUNGEON STAIRWAY *winds through the papal Castel Sant' Angelo, which Cesare Borgia used both as a home and a prison. Here, according to rumor, he often did away with four or five enemies a day.*

A STATELY FOUR-POSTER, *draped with a gown, adorns Lucrezia's bedroom in her castle near Rome. Her huge wardrobe included 50 gowns, 20 hats, 33 pairs of shoes, 60 pairs of slippers and 20 mantles.*

WORKSHOPS OF TWO BOLD SPIRITS

Andrea Mantegna, a painter, and Aldus Manutius, a printer, exemplified the boldness of the Renaissance. Mantegna, taken into the painters' guild of Padua at 10, mastered and exploited new techniques of perspective; his foreshortened portrait of the dead Christ, which made the Savior look almost like a cadaver, shocked and astounded all who saw it. A daring experimenter in painting, Mantegna also turned to other media; in his studio *(opposite)*, he helped perfect the new art of copper engraving.

Aldus Manutius was the foremost printer in Italy. In the earliest days of printing, he published hundreds of compact and inexpensive volumes. Many men of the time, like the Duke of Urbino, would not let the new printed books into their libraries. But Manutius, turning out everything from contemporary poetry to 2,000-year-old Greek classics, was not deterred. "Those who cultivate letters must be supplied with . . . books," he declared, ". . . and until this supply is secure I shall not rest."

AN EARLY PRESS, *like the one owned by Aldus Manutius, used primitive printing techniques to produce magnificent books. Pages were set in type by hand, inked, and run off one at a time on the wooden press. Copies were then hung up to dry.*

A WORKSHOP OF GENIUS, *Andrea Mantegna's studio in Mantua (opposite) is cluttered with his drawings and engraving tools. The bronze bust at center was done in classical style, reflecting Mantegna's love of the art of ancient Rome.*

5

THE TRIUMPH OF ART

We have seen that Italy was the most variously alert of European states, and that Florence, among the Italian states, was the chief pioneer in intellectual and cultural life. Now we come to the aspect of its leadership that has provided the most lasting pleasure and inspiration to posterity—the revolution in the fine arts which Florence began and pushed through to a triumphant conclusion.

Between the careers of two great Florentines, Giotto and Michelangelo, Italian artists moved from the unrealistic and symbolic art of the Middle Ages to a mastery of illusion—to an art which gave the impression that it was an accurate representation of the real world. The movement began in Florence and enjoyed most of its development there. It was given its momentum by three crucial generations. The first, at the beginning of the 14th Century, was dominated by Giotto. The chief names in the second, in the early 15th Century, are those of the painter Masaccio and the sculptor Donatello. The third, which spanned the late 15th and early 16th Centuries, was notable for Leonardo da Vinci and Raphael, and culminated in Michelangelo, who, as his fellow painter Vasari said, not only copied nature to perfection, but went beyond nature to produce an ideal, intensely personal vision: "He used to make figures nine, ten, even twelve heads high, simply to increase their grace. He would say that the artist must have his measuring tools in the eye, rather than in the hand, as it is the eye that judges."

Giotto, who took the first giant step in this development, was a genuine revolutionary. There was little in the work of any previous painter to help him achieve space that looked like real space, or human figures that expressed human emotions. The medieval painter had looked at the world through a window frosted by conventions; the warmth of Giotto's outlook melted most of them away. To medieval man a painting of a man was "real" in that it reminded him of a real man, much as a child's portrait of his father is "real" to him even if it is only a stick figure. Both are allusions to reality. Giotto turned away from this symbolic world to paint in a manner that made direct statements about people and things. His men stand in lifelike positions and groups, interrelated as real men are when they are conversing or watching some spectacle. His settings are rational attempts to portray real rooms and real space. What possessed Giotto to paint in this way, no one knows. Perhaps there is some truth to the legend that he started life as a goatherd, living far from the influence of medieval painters, and was therefore able to record what he saw according to his own instincts—instincts similar to those of the prehistoric men who painted moving animals on the walls of their caves with the precision and skill of huntsmen who had to know their quarry.

Whatever the motivation, Giotto's art spoke to some need in the society of his day. Those who saw his work in Assisi, Rome, Padua, Naples and Florence had to be for or against him; he could not be ignored. Dante, in his *Purgatory*, noted that Giotto's predecessor Cimabue "thought that he held the field in painting, but now Giotto is acclaimed." Giovanni Villani praised his fellow citizen as "the most sovereign master of painting in his time, who drew all his figures and their postures according to nature," and added that "he was given a salary by the commune in virtue of his talent and his excellence." Later Leonardo da Vinci made the same point when he wrote that "the painter will produce pictures of small merit if he takes for his standard the pictures of others, but if he will study from natural objects he will bear good fruit." He instanced Giotto, who "being born in the mountains and in a solitude inhabited only by goats and such beasts, and being guided by nature to his art, began by drawing on the rocks the movements of the goats of which he was keeper."

Leonardo went on to say that "Afterwards this art declined again, because everyone imitated the pictures that were already done . . . until Masaccio showed by his perfect works how those who take for their standard anyone but nature—the mistress of all masters—weary themselves in vain." Masaccio,

the first painter after Giotto to approach him in talent, lived in the early 15th Century. With him, painting entered a period of intense technical development, most of which is foreshadowed in the work of Masaccio himself. His figures are both more solid and more relaxed than Giotto's, and his settings are imbued with a sense of moving air. He was the first Renaissance painter to master the use of mechanical perspective, the first to indicate human anatomy under the folds of draperies and the first to experiment intensively with chiaroscuro—a way of painting shadows so as to give definition to the forms they fall across. All three of these—but especially perspective—were to occupy the attention of painters and sculptors for the next 50 years.

Mechanical perspective was probably invented by the architect Brunelleschi, who may have stumbled upon its principles in the course of his studies of the proportions of ancient Roman buildings. His discovery enormously excited his fellow artists. Some, like Masaccio, made masterful use of it, and others became obsessed by it. Paolo Uccello, a contemporary of Masaccio's, became so intrigued with its techniques that he stayed at his drawing table all night, replying to his wife when she asked him to come to bed, "Oh, what a delightful thing is this perspective!" And Piero della Francesca went back to the Greek mathematicians for theoretical support, in order to write a treatise on perspective which helped even second-rate painters to draw the relative size of objects correctly.

By the time of Leonardo, painters had become so skilled in the use of perspective drawing that Leonardo could use two perspectives simultaneously—some of the *Mona Lisa's* air of mystery comes from the fact that the figure and her background are constructed on two different vanishing points.

Stimulated by mechanical perspective, painters also investigated aerial perspective, using progressively paler colors on receding objects to obtain a

PRINCIPLES OF PERSPECTIVE, *a study that fascinated Renaissance artists, are demonstrated in these illustrations. The street scene at top, sketched by the Sienese painter and architect Baldassare Peruzzi, shows how perspective conveys an illusion of depth on a flat surface. At bottom, in a simplified version of the sketch, superimposed white lines follow Peruzzi's principal lines, converging at a single "vanishing point" (center). Artists of the Renaissance carefully plotted such converging lines as a guide before they executed a painting.*

sense of distance. And from chiaroscuro the manipulation of light and shade along the edges of a form evolved into *sfumato*, a blurring or hazing of the outline of an object to blend it into its surroundings. Leonardo, who pioneered in the use of *sfumato*, also discovered that shadows are not gray, but have color—that on snow, for example, they are blue. Similarly, Masaccio's painterly interest in anatomy flowered into something a good deal more. A preoccupation with the construction of the human body led painters to the study of anatomy. One of them, Antonio Pollaiuolo, drew bodies with such precise muscle structure that he is believed to be the first artist actually to practice dissection of corpses. His famous engraving, *Battle of Nude Men*, probably had much to do with the establishment later on of a vogue for painting the body in violent, sometimes contorted action, with every sinew and muscle showing. Not until the 19th Century French Impressionists did any group of artists make a greater contribution toward reproducing nature on a flat surface.

And yet Renaissance art did not move toward this goal unfalteringly. Despite the fact that many of its patrons were laymen, most of the art remained religious art—and men require different things of religion at different times. When life is calm and prosperous they think of Christ and the saints as friends and want them portrayed as such —that is, as virtual mortals; they will even accept idealized versions of a painter's wife or mistress as the Virgin. But when times are troubled, men think of death and the Day of Judgment and want Christ and the saints portrayed as intercessors, inscrutable and divine.

Something of the sort happened in the middle of the 14th Century, when the Black Death swept over Italy. Giotto and his followers, with their emphasis on the humanity of the Biblical characters and stories, were cast aside and a new kind of painting became popular. It emphasized the miraculous and the authoritarian: to save men from death a miracle was needed; to nerve them for the ordeal of death they needed the support of the Church. Suddenly the differences between Christ and mortal men, between the Virgin and ordinary women, became more important than their similarities.

In this new painting the Virgin no longer sits on the ground, holding her Baby like any other mother, but hovers supernaturally in the air. Christ is not shown in humanity, but in majesty, dressed in clothes of glittering splendor beyond the means of mortal men; He stands not in a rational landscape but in enigmatic space. Painters turn to new or rarely used themes that have intimations of immortality—the Trinity, the Pentecost. And Biblical subjects which Giotto and his followers had treated almost as genre paintings—such as the Virgin's presentation at the temple—become rigid and hieratical. Instead of moving impulsively up the temple steps, Mary is frozen into a symbol of the soul seeking salvation and redemption; the priest awaiting her does not turn to greet her, but instead stares out at the spectator: "Without me," he seems to intone, "you cannot be saved." Figures which at the beginning of the century had been shown in the attitudes of ordinary men now stand stiffly and their faces, regressing to a medieval convention, are shown frontally or in sharp profile.

But by 1380 the panic was over. Men plucked up the courage to face life on earth again, and painters picked up the thread of realism which fear and mysticism had made them drop. Toward the century's close an insipid but lifelike painter, Spinello Aretino, brought human emotion and representational accuracy back into painting, and in doing so revived the movement which Giotto had begun—and which was now to run unchecked for more than a hundred years. But the real turning point was not so much Spinello's pallid paintings

BRONZE CASTING, *the art illustrated here as Benvenuto Cellini used it in making his statue of Perseus, was done by the "cire-perdue," or "lost wax" process. (1) The sculptor modeled a figure of clay (shown in black), which he coated with wax (light section). Metal pins were used to hold everything in place. (2) The figure was encased in plaster. As heat was applied, the wax melted and ran out through numerous vents at the bottom of the mold.*

3

4

MOLTEN METAL *was poured into the plaster mold (3). The bronze filled up the space left empty when the melted wax had poured out (heavy line). After the metal had cooled and hardened, the sculptor chiseled away the plaster (4). The projecting pins were cut off and the inner core of clay was removed. Finally, Cellini polished his completed statue of Perseus and added, as he said, "some trifles of gold, varnish and various other little finishings."*

as it was another event: the competition, in 1401, for the selection of an artist to design a pair of bronze doors for the Baptistery of Florence. In the competition two of Florence's most respected sculptors, Filippo Brunelleschi and Lorenzo Ghiberti, were rivals, and the closeness of the contest engaged the interest of all of Florence.

The conditions set by the merchant guild which had commissioned the doors plainly had only esthetic considerations in mind. "It was determined," Vasari wrote in his life of the winner, Ghiberti, "that the scene represented should be the sacrifice of Isaac by Abraham, which was considered to be a good subject in which the masters could grapple with the difficulties of the art, because it comprises a landscape, figures both nude and draped, and animals, while the figures in the foreground might be made in full relief, those in the middle distance in half-relief, and those in the background in bas-relief." Ghiberti's piece was chosen over Brunelleschi's because, says Vasari, "the whole scene was well designed and the composition excellent, the figures being slender and graceful, the pose admirable and so beautifully finished that it did not look as if it had been cast and polished, but rather as if it had been created by a breath."

In short, apart from the superior unity of Ghiberti's mood, the judges gave the prize to the design that showed, not the most spiritual intensity, but the most attention to the classical nude.

As with Giotto, almost a century before, Ghiberti's artistic thinking coincided with public taste. Humanism, which gave him and his fellow artists an increasing body of esthetic theory to draw upon for support, also gave them an increasingly cultivated and sophisticated body of patrons. Not that humanism was without rivals. There were still painters like Gentile da Fabriano and Benozzo Gozzoli, painting beautifully colored, medieval-inspired scenes crowded with elegant attenuated figures—looking much like exquisite miniatures blown up to fresco size. But this bright and intellectually languid style was not truly Tuscan; it was an import from the aristocratic Burgundian courts to the north. The true Tuscan style, the style that was by degrees to transform art not only in Italy but all over Europe, was the creation of Florence.

By about 1425 Masaccio had put the seal on this new style with his magnificently controlled painting of the Trinity in the church of Santa Maria Novella, in which God the Father does not float in the empyrean but stands firmly beneath the vault, not of heaven, but of a splendidly drawn Roman arch. By the same year Brunelleschi, putting aside his disappointment over the outcome of the Baptistery door competition, had turned his attention exclusively to architecture and designed the Innocenti Foundling Hospital, using classical proportions. And by the same year Ghiberti was at work on the last pair of Baptistery doors, modeling his figures with such skill that Michelangelo is reported to have declared, some 50 years later, that they were fit to be the doors to Paradise. Harmony, gravity, logic were the order of the day, and the art theorist Alberti was able to despise those ignorant painters—the painters of wedding chests and others—who continued to use real gold in their work to achieve a tricky and ostentatious glitter.

Yet despite this intense drive toward realism Renaissance art did not, in one sense, actually copy nature. Reality is a word with many shades of meaning. The figures of Giotto are real compared to the figures in earlier art, but seem less so when compared to those of Raphael, 200 years later. By Raphael's time scientific studies enabled artists to copy nature with great verisimilitude—systems of perspective had been worked out and the human body had been examined, dead and alive, at close range. But the sense of a painting's reality is never

the result of scientific tricks. No great realistic painting is ever great because it is an exact copy of something. The representation of reality is not art unless it is strongly infused with the changes and choices made by the eye that looked upon nature's original. But the more convinced we are that an artist *could* produce an exact copy of an object if he chose, the more acutely we become aware of how his vision differs from a coldly photographic one.

So it was with the Renaissance artist's scientific studies. While they helped him copy nature, at the same time they tempted him away from what he actually saw. Perspective, for example, formidably rational and mathematical though it was, was merely an artificial method of representing space. It assumed a fixed viewpoint and a fixed eye, and was therefore a device. And like every device in painting, it tempted the creative artist to play with it. Uccello, in his battle pieces, played with it in the interest of decorative pattern-making; Leonardo, in the *Mona Lisa*, played with it to evoke an atmosphere of mystery.

Similarly with anatomy. Signorelli repeatedly redrew the limbs of his figures to make them look like real people (the successive versions are still visible in his drawings), but Michelangelo, in his nudes—especially in the *Last Judgment*—contorted reality to give his figures an inner expressiveness. Even Alberti, a fervent propagandist for the imitation of nature, sometimes wrote from an urge that seemed directed more toward beauty than truth: "We have set down the principal measurements of a man," he noted in his book on sculpture. "We did not, however, choose this or that single body, but . . . have tried to note and set down in writing the highest beauty scattered, as if in calculated portions, among many bodies."

It was in rebuttal to this use of nature to surpass nature that Leonardo remarked: "that painting is the most to be praised which agrees most exactly with the thing imitated." Leonardo thought that the painter should refer constantly to what was before his eyes—as the young Giotto had—and not to his memory. He should not use the raw material of nature to extract the ideal from it. And it was in rebuttal to this thesis that Michelangelo, in turn, saw the artist's aim not as an imitation of nature, nor as an idealization based on a collection of the best of this and that, but as an expression of an ideal present in his own mind.

Neither were the Renaissance artists concerned with the kind of realism that strives to make scenes real in the sense of being lifelike. No Renaissance artist ever painted a landscape for its own sake, or a group of people engaged in informal conversation. Painters were seldom troubled by the anachronism of introducing contemporary figures into Biblical scenes, seldom troubled by any notion of *verismo*, "truth to life." In this respect a medieval characteristic—the period's tolerance of

the simultaneous existence of reality and unreality in its paintings—lingered on.

Renaissance realism was also qualified by another medieval trait: the persistent use of symbols to comment on or explain the meaning of a painting. If anything, Renaissance painting, in spite of its realistic appearance, became even more mystical in its message than medieval art. The ability to copy nature accurately enabled its painters to use symbols more precisely, and to use more of them. Symbols lurk in the most naturalistic looking scenes. In fact, Renaissance art cannot be understood—neither the aims of those who produced it, nor the reactions of those who looked at it—without understanding this. The goldfinch in St. John's hand in Raphael's *Madonna of the Goldfinch* is not just a pretty bird, it is a symbol of fertility: the painting was done as a wedding gift from the artist to his friend Lorenzo Nasi. And the goldfinch could mean other things, too. It could symbolize the soul or—following the legend that

Christ as a child had brought clay birds to life—the Resurrection. Sometimes it became a symbol for the Passion, alluding to another legend which told how a little bird flew down and pulled a thorn from Christ's brow while he was carrying the cross.

Indeed it was common for paintings of the Holy Family to carry the onlooker's mind forward to the Passion—and vice versa. In his *Pietà* in St. Peter's, Michelangelo accomplishes this by contrasting the dead Christ with a youthful Mary; she is of an age to dandle a baby rather than to hold a man on her lap. Conversely, in Michelangelo's painting of the Holy Family, the gesture with which Joseph hands down the Christ Child to His mother is not merely a charming domestic touch, but a reference to the lifting down of Christ from the Cross. To emphasize this point, Michelangelo includes the figure of a youthful Bacchus, the pagan god of wine, in the background. Henceforth, the picture says, mystical ecstasy is not dependent on the wine of pagan revels, but on the wine which represents the blood of Christ.

Similarly, Leonardo's drawing of the *Virgin and St. Anne* in the British Museum is a good deal more than the relaxed family scene it appears to be on the surface. The Christ Child is shown blessing St. John. And while Mary looks indulgently at the two children, St. Anne, with her upward-pointing finger, forewarns that the Child will be crucified. Finally, by placing the Virgin on St. Anne's knee, Leonardo makes the point that the whole process of redemption is contained within the Church, of which St. Anne is the symbol. Within this reference, St. Anne's warning and sympathetic glance are reminders that in spite of sadness, hope can come to all mankind if it will accept the Church's teaching.

In fact, the Church's teaching is sometimes the very heart of the symbolism. Raphael's painting of the *Dispute on the Nature of the Sacrament*, for instance, illustrates the Church's position in a theological argument that raged in Raphael's time. Reformers like John Wyclif in England and Jan Hus in Bohemia had said that the wafer and wine of the Eucharist were not strictly speaking the body and blood of Christ and did not have to be blessed by a priest. But Raphael's painting, commissioned by the Vatican, says otherwise. The sacrament sits on an altar in the center of the picture, flanked on one side by the illustrious Church Fathers whose writings have concentrated on the Eucharist's meaning to men's daily lives, and on the other side by the theologians who understand its inner, mystical meaning. Once more an upward-pointing finger—this time on a figure beside the altar—indicates the risen Christ and sums up what the argument is all about.

Only recently the same gesture has led to a new interpretation of the meaning of Leonardo's *Last Supper*. In this painting the finger is that of St. Thomas, who sits directly next to Christ Himself. The conventional explanation of his pointing gesture, along with the gestures and expressions of all the other apostles, was that they were reacting to Christ's statement, "One among you will betray me." But their reactions are much more believable if we understand that Christ has just said, "Take, eat; this is my Body which is given for you," and "Drink . . . for this is my Blood of the New Testament." This does not rule out the previous interpretation—the consciousness of betrayal—since without the betrayal there could have been no crucifixion. In fact the similarity in gesture between Christ's and Judas' outstretched hands makes this very connection. But the new interpretation subordinates this theme to that of the nature of the sacraments —an idea much more profound and moving.

It was a commonplace in the theological literature of the time that any text in the Bible could be interpreted in four ways: in its literal sense, as

CULTURES AT FAR ENDS OF THE EARTH

During the same centuries that saw the unfolding of the Renaissance in Europe, two great civilizations—the Aztec in Mexico and the Ming Dynasty in China—rose and flourished. Aztecs controlled the entire valley of Mexico by the mid-15th Century. Their capital, Tenochtitlán (now Mexico City), was a city of about 100,000 people, its streets ornamented with rich art like the sculpture of Coatlicue, goddess of earth and death, at left. Then in 1521, the Spaniard Hernán Cortés captured Tenochtitlán, and brought Aztec rule to an end.

In China, an uprising in 1368 had replaced Mongol overlords with a purely Chinese government which favored the arts. For nearly 300 years Peking was the center of a magnificent culture still famed for exquisitely thin porcelains and for beautifully painted scrolls of landscapes. The "Forbidden City" at Peking, with its celebrated pagodas, waterways and courtyards, was erected by Ming Dynasty architects.

evidence of a moral law, as a mystical promise, and as a key to salvation. Leonardo's grouping of the disciples follows this idea. He has divided them into four groups of three men each. On the far right is a group whose hands are outstretched to accept the Eucharistic key; the enraptured group next to them responds to the mystical promise; the group to the immediate left of Christ copes with the literal implication of His words—that is, that He must die; and the group on the far left expresses anger and horror that the moral law makes this demand of their Master. A reasonably well-educated Renaissance viewer would also have connected the connotations in this first Eucharist with a commonly believed medical theory, derived from antiquity, that a man's temperament is determined by the balance of four "humors": phlegm, associated with quiet acceptance; blood, with optimism; melancholy, with thoughtfulness; and choler, with anger. Each

group of disciples appears to be dominated by one or another of these humors; only one figure, that of Christ, contains them all in perfect balance; only His body can be perfect spirit, and man can become perfect only in Him.

Thus, the *Last Supper* made its impact not only through its noble naturalism and its compositional grace and energy, but as commentary on the central doctrine of the Church. It is a superb painting as well as a piece of graphic theology. There are similar theological lessons in many Renaissance paintings, even in those that seem to be wholly secular and sensuous. Titian's nude and clothed Venuses in *Sacred and Profane Love*, for instance, represent not only the two poles of Platonic beauty (the nude being the higher, because truth dares to be naked) but the two kinds of Christian love, the love of God and the love of one's neighbor, which together constitute the highest Christian virtue, Charity.

As the Renaissance wore on, the meaning behind the appearance of objects became increasingly elaborate. The more skillfully the artists represented reality, the more reluctant they were to stop there.

For centuries scholars have puzzled over the meaning behind the two tombs which Michelangelo designed for Giuliano and Lorenzo de' Medici (not Lorenzo the Magnificent, but his grandson) in the Medici Chapel in the church of San Lorenzo. About the symbolism of the chapel as a whole, which Michelangelo also designed, there is little disagreement. It represents the three zones of man's existence: heaven, earth and Hades. The statues of the two princes are set in the middle zone of earth, in niches above the tombs where their souls lie— in Hades—awaiting God's decision whether to free them or not. Both princes turn their heads to watch a statue of the Virgin and Child on the wall between them, hoping for a sign that they will rise to heaven, which is suggested by a zone of light created by the chapel's windows just below the dome.

The symbolism of the tombs themselves has almost as many interpretations as interpreters. Architecturally they are similar to palace façades, a reference perhaps to the ancient idea of the tomb as the house of the dead. Their decorations are the ancient Roman emblems associated with death and immortality—garlands, jars of oil, shells, dolphins, allegorical masks. But the princes are not dead; they rest in the house of death—having left one life, they await another. The statue of Giuliano holds in his hand several oboloi, the traditional coins of Hades; Lorenzo leans his elbow on a box covered with a bat's head, the bird of Hades. The chapel is ringed with blind doors, apparently the doors to Hades, through which, as Vergil wrote in the *Aeneid*, it was easy to pass but difficult to return. Two figures recline on each tomb, *Evening* and *Dawn* on Lorenzo's, *Night* and *Day* on Giuliano's, symbols not only of the four times of day, but also—since

they resemble the ancient Roman river gods—of the four rivers of Hades. These reclining figures have slipped aside to let the dead men rise a little way to their niches on the wall—beautiful, eternally young, but waiting. Even time is slowed: *Dawn* wakes with anguish; *Day* shields himself from the sun as from an assassin. Lorenzo and Giuliano—and those of us who watch them—are left to ponder the soul's fate, midway in passage between death and eternal life.

Sometimes the symbolism of 16th Century artists must have defeated even the most learned of their viewers. To understand the Medici Chapel fully, Michelangelo's contemporaries would have to have read Plato's dialogue on immortality, the *Phaedo*, as well as the Bible. And who could have known, without Vasari's own written commentary, that the gleam on the armor in Vasari's painting of Alessandro de' Medici represented Alessandro's reflections on the interests of his subjects? Or that the ruined house in the painting's background refers to the Medici's exile? Or that Alessandro sits on a circular seat because circles have no end—and neither would the rule of the Medici family? Or that the bit of purple fabric on Alessandro's knee is a reference to the murdered Giuliano de' Medici? No one. Symbolism had gone beyond teaching into the realm of intellectual whimsy.

In the final analysis the urge to allegorize, to load the simple with symbolic overtones, to make something stand for something else, was as strong in the 15th and 16th Centuries as it had been in the Middle Ages. Realism, the unvarnished realism of the kitchen sink or the cluttered attic, was alien to Renaissance tastes. Their art only looks straightforward to us because we cannot read the clues. In fact, it is a tribute to the strength of their naturalism that it did not break down under the weight of symbolic overtones—that Leonardo and Michelangelo can still make us think we are seeing quite possible people behaving in quite believable ways.

A NEW NATURALISM, *preparing the way for the Renaissance, appears in Giotto's fresco "The Meeting of Joachim and Anna at the Golden Gate."*

THE MASTERWORKS

The deep interest in man which characterized the Renaissance found lasting expression in the art of the age. No other epoch has brought together so many great painters, sculptors and architects. From the moment when the 14th Century painter Giotto broke with medieval tradition to emphasize man's natural instead of his spiritual aspect *(above)*, art was never again the same. To the artists themselves the Renaissance was an age of tremendous change, of radical advances in technique. Each painting became a technical challenge, an adventure in perspective, a revolution in the use of color. A few artists worked alone; most ran busy shops, full of assistants and apprentices, often crowded with prospective customers. Increasingly, all found the human figure the noblest subject for their art.

A COMMANDING CHRIST *dominates Masaccio's fresco "The Tribute Money." Molded by light and shadow, Masaccio's figures gain depth.*

MASTERS OF THE NEW REALISM

The new realism heralded by Giotto was dramatically advanced in the 15th Century by three great Florentines, Brunelleschi, Masaccio and Donatello —and brought to its height by the Umbrian Piero della Francesca. Brunelleschi scientifically plotted the laws of linear perspective for the first time— applying mathematics he had learned from Toscanelli, who also counseled Christopher Columbus. Masaccio added effects of light and shadings of color to heighten perspective, portraying figures that appear fully "in the round." By the end of the century, painters were so enthralled with perspective that, as Piero della Francesca observed, measurement had become as important to art as drawing. Artists talked of points, lines and angles, and described their subjects in terms of squares and cubes and tetragons. Others pioneered in anatomical studies: Donatello, for one, created the first nude sculptures since antiquity. The goal of each artist was the same: the mastery of realism.

THE PAZZI CHAPEL, *designed by Brunelleschi about 1430, is proportioned according to the architect's own measurement of ancient Roman buildings.*

DONATELLO'S ST. GEORGE *gazes ahead with such confident ease that when Michelangelo first saw the statue, he said: "March!"*

"THE RESURRECTION," *a fresco by Piero della Francesca, reveals the strong sense of design typical of this painter-mathematician.*

"THE LAST JUDGMENT," *a virtuoso display of anatomy, was painted by Luca Signorelli. In this Renaissance hell, even the demons are human.*

EXPRESSIONS OF GREATER ARTISTIC FREEDOM

One generation of Florentine masters showed how the human figure could be naturalistically fixed in space; the next made its figures move. At the end of the 15th Century, Antonio del Pollaiuolo *(left, below)* set athletic figures in violent motion, showing every muscle strained. In the paintings of Luca Signorelli *(left, above)*, which Michelangelo studied before designing his own frescoes for the Sistine Chapel, every posture of the body in action is shown. In Mantegna's *Dead Christ (far right, below)*, unusual perspective makes even repose seem restless.

Besides introducing movement to art, the later generations of Renaissance masters expanded its subject matter. Botticelli painted not only religious subjects but also ancient myths and allegories *(right)*. Piero di Cosimo filled his landscapes *(below)* with Stone Age men and primitive beasts.

"HERCULES AND ANTEUS," *a bronze study of violent stress, is by Antonio del Pollaiuolo, one of the first artists to dissect a cadaver.*

A SCATHING ALLEGORY by Botticelli portrays Calumny, flanked by Fraud, Treason and Envy, dragging a youthful victim before an ass-eared king.

A STONE AGE SCENE, showing a hunter amid real and fanciful animals, is one of six panels of prehistoric life executed by Piero di Cosimo.

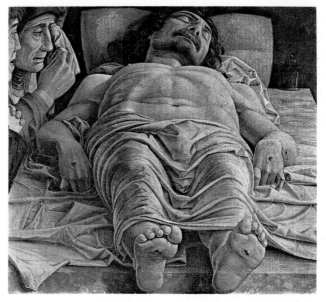

"THE DEAD CHRIST," in startling perspective, was painted by Mantegna partly as an exercise in the technique of foreshortening.

THE CA' D'ORO, *a 15th Century Venetian palace, blends Gothic and Saracen design. Gold leaf originally covered its marble façade.*

"SACRED AND PROFANE LOVE," *an allegorical painting of about 1515 by Titian, illustrates how, by applying the techniques of Venetian painting,*

A PASTORAL SCENE, *Giorgione's celebration of musicians and nudes was painted about 1508, two years before the young artist died of plague.*

this master was able to depict a wide variety of textures with great realism: flesh, satin, sky and the marble relief of the fountain.

SAINT FRANCIS IN ECSTASY, *a panel painted by Giovanni Bellini about 1480, shows the Venetian artist's use of oils to create lustrous lighting.*

THE SPLENDORS OF VENETIAN ART

As Florence was the birthplace of form in Renaissance art, Venice was the home of color. The father of Venetian art, Giovanni Bellini, had begun to experiment with oil glazes in the last quarter of the 15th Century. Until then, tempera—pigments mixed with egg yolk—had been employed in Italian painting almost exclusively. Oil glaze added luster. Pupils of Bellini, Giorgione (*opposite*) and Titian (*above*) produced paintings remarkable for their blending of rich tones. During his long career, Titian further explored the use of oils and developed a technique known as impasto—using thin layers of opaque pigment and oil glazes to give his colors a new subtlety and depth. Titian's art enthralled his patrons, but purists of the Florentine school found fault. When Michelangelo, a Florentine, saw Titian's works in Rome, he remarked that although he admired the Venetian's "coloring and style, it was a pity good design was not taught in Venice."

A BRONZE GODDESS, *in a relief by Alessandro Leopardi, adorns one of the flagstaff pedestals he designed for the Piazza San Marco in Venice. Venetian sculpture tended to be more decorative than monumental.*

RAPHAEL'S MADONNA *with Christ and St. John the Baptist, paint-*
ed when the artist was in his early twenties, shows figures ar-
ranged in a pyramid—a design Raphael borrowed from Leonardo.

ST. PETER'S DOME, *designed by Michelangelo, rises*
above paired columns nearly 50 feet high to a
total height, stressed by vertical ribs, of 452 feet.

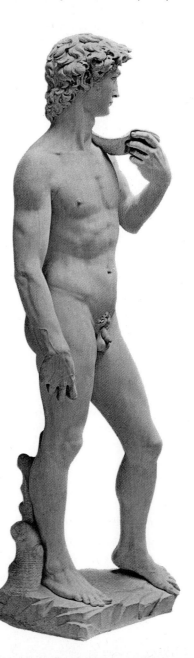

PREPARED FOR BATTLE, *Michelangelo's "David" expresses vibrant*
power harmoniously contained. Completed in 1504, it is the
crowning work of the great tradition initiated by Donatello.

"THE LAST SUPPER" *by Leonardo da Vinci, from which this detail is taken, reveals—although pocked and repainted—the artist's mastery of design.*

THE FINAL TRIUMPH OF TECHNIQUE

In a score of years, between 1500 and 1520, three men of genius lifted Italian art to its summit. Leonardo da Vinci opened the way. A master of perspective, shading and color, he created lifelike figures with mere half strokes, blurred outlines, or shadowy features. Raphael shared Leonardo's dream of depicting ideal beauty, and the nearly geometrical grace of his paintings brought this ideal to perfection. Raphael embodied the rational poise of the High Renaissance. Michelangelo's colossal statues challenged this equilibrium with a turbulent energy that gave life to the very stone.

THE ERA OF MANNERISM

The aftermath of the High Renaissance was 16th Century Mannerism. Turning from nature and classical ideals, Mannerist painters dramatized the stress of their own emotions. Pontormo manipulated anatomy and dissolved space; Parmigianino elongated forms and turned perspective—once the artist's pride—into a jarring puzzle.

Tintoretto was an innovator who felt he was carrying on the traditions of the past. A sign at his studio proclaimed: "The drawing of Michelangelo and the color of Titian." Yet the paintings by Tintoretto (*opposite*) are utterly unlike any that had come before. Known to his contemporaries as *il furioso* for his amazing speed, Tintoretto added to art a fervor and a sweeping use of impasto all his own. His was a new art, as brilliant as it was violent.

"THE MADONNA OF THE LONG NECK," *by Parmigianino, shows human forms pulled out of proportion to satisfy the artist's fascination with a variety of geometrical forms. Here, necks and legs stretch into long cylinders.*

MANNERED POSES *and unnatural colors abound in Jacopo da Pontormo's "The Deposition," painted about 1528. Figures are contorted to fit the oval design.*

A SUPPLE PERSEUS *holds Medusa's head in this bronze by Benvenuto Cellini. Although Cellini remained closer to nature than most Mannerists, the aging Michelangelo dismissed his sculptures as "snuff-box ornaments."*

A STUDY IN CONTRASTS, *Tintoretto's "Abduction of the Body of Saint Mark"* is eerily lit and plunged far back in perspective. The tranquil geometry of pavement and arches makes the action seem doubly turbulent.

6

A CREATIVE ELITE

One of the most extraordinary phenomena in the history of art was the rebirth, after the Middle Ages, of the desire to reproduce the real world in paint and marble and bronze. But alongside this phenomenon another appeared, almost equally extraordinary: the change in social status of the artist. In the Middle Ages painters and sculptors had been craftsmen like other craftsmen, no different in kind from carpenters or bakers. The Renaissance saw the rise of the modern idea of the artist as an individual, a genius to be judged by standards different from those applied to ordinary men.

Humanism, a devotion to classical art and literature, was largely responsible for this. However much it may have hampered the artist's instinctive self-expression it changed him, by educating him, from a craftsman into a man of learning. Some of this learning was acquired from theoretical texts on esthetics, but a great deal of it was acquired through direct contact with ancient statues and buildings—and nowhere were these more in evidence than in Rome.

Many artists went to Rome. Two of the earliest to make the pilgrimage were the Florentines Donatello and Brunelleschi. For the latter the trip was partly an escape; he had just lost the competition for the design of the bronze doors of the Baptistery of Florence. "Neither was bothered by family cares and worries," wrote the contemporary chronicler Manetti, "because neither had a wife or children there or elsewhere." Also, foreshadowing the bohemian behavior that later became the mark of artistic genius, "Neither was much concerned with how he ate, drank, lived or dressed himself, provided he could satisfy himself with these things to see and measure."

Donatello amassed a collection of ancient coins and gems, but the most valuable thing the two brought back to Florence was enthusiasm for the culture they had unearthed. Other artists followed their lead in collecting art objects, notably Lorenzo Ghiberti, the winner of the Baptistery door competition. So, too, did some of the foremost humanist scholars and art patrons of the day. Niccolò Niccoli —who "patronized painters, sculptors and architects as well as men of letters, and had a thorough knowledge of their crafts"—collected statuary,

A PORTRAIT OF A YOUTH, *attributed to Filippino Lippi, captures the boy's individuality but also idealizes his features. Renaissance artists generally sought to follow Aristotle's precept—"Paint people better than they are."*

coins and gems, as well as manuscripts. Leon Battista Alberti, infected by the Roman example, designed the most meticulously "classical" building in Florence, the Palazzo Rucellai. But Alberti did not stop there. So closely did he identify himself with the antique spirit that he was able to write—and pass off as genuine—a comedy purported to be by a Roman writer. In the same manner the young Michelangelo fooled connoisseurs with an "antique" marble cupid.

Of all the men affected by antiquity, however, the ones who were influenced most were probably the architects. Architecture, founded, in the words of the scholar Marsilio Ficino, on "the eternal truths" of geometry, was the least subjective of the arts. An architect of the Renaissance could tap the glory of Rome's pagan greatness, learn from the proportions, engineering and details of its buildings, without playing traitor to the Christian spirit of his own time. Even so, he was seldom a direct copyist. There were no Roman models for church façades and *palazzi*, and he did not always choose to use such models as there were. The Renaissance preferred, for example, the tall dome of Byzantine architecture to the shallow dome of Rome's Pantheon. And although Brunelleschi and his contemporaries carefully measured such details as capitals and pediments, they used these details with great freedom. The churches of Brunelleschi are uniquely his own, despite their debt to the Roman basilica and to such Roman details as arch, pillar, capital and coffering.

As for Renaissance sculptors, they were influenced as much by the experiments of contemporary painters as they were by the statues of Rome. Although one sculptor working in Giotto's time, Nicola Pisano, derived his naturalistic style from the influence of Roman sculpture, most of his successors took their naturalism from the paintings of Giotto. For more than a hundred years, from An-

A RENAISSANCE NOTION OF ROME, *this print of the Baths of Diocletian offers an imaginative—and highly inaccurate—return to classicism: the basic Roman design is embellished with medieval columns and Renaissance frame windows.*

drea Pisano's first set of doors for the Florentine Baptistery in 1336 to Ghiberti's second set in 1452, sculptors tried to give their reliefs the same sense of real space and rational communication between the figures that Giotto had given his paintings.

Even Donatello's fascination with Roman statues was limited to using them for ideas about what sculpture should do rather than how it should be done. His famous statue of Gattamelata astride his horse, in Padua, owes something to the classical statue of Marcus Aurelius on horseback, in Rome, but the brooding inwardness of his *Judith and Holofernes*, in Florence, is far removed from the classical temperament. So also is his *Mary Magdalen* in the Florentine Baptistery. Although the statue's mastery of form may have been learned from observing antiquity, all traces of Donatello's antiquarian research have been obliterated by the *Magdalen*'s scorchingly personal style.

In fact the ancient world was influencing men already inclined to turn their backs on the Middle Ages—men whose fresh outlook had made it impossible for them to go on reproducing medieval art, however glorious. The classical freestanding nude helped sculptors already disposed to see the human figure in the round. Roman doors and windows appealed to architects whose mathematical interests had already led them to reject the pointed Gothic arch for the rational geometry of semicircles and squares. "Apart from the weakness of a pointed arch, it lacks the grace of our style, which is pleasing to the eye because of the perfection of a circle," says a report on the monuments of ancient Rome. Its authors, who were probably Castiglione and Raphael, add, with a nod to the other main influence on Renaissance art, "It may be observed that nature itself strives for no other form."

This same report also contains a bitter denunciation of the popes for allowing the monuments of ancient Rome to decay into fodder for lime kilns:

"How much of all this new Rome that we see today," the authors ask Leo X, "however great, however beautiful, however adorned with palaces and churches and other buildings, has been built with lime made from ancient marbles?" Interest in the marbles, indeed in all Roman art and architecture, had grown ever more intense. As if to protect themselves from the limitations of realism, artists were seizing on an art that was spiritually larger than life—more ordered, more graceful, more heroic. At the same time a succession of truly magnificent finds emerged from the darkness to astonish and excite them.

One of these was the statue of the *Laocoön*, a marvel of the Hellenistic Age. Another, the so-called *Belvedere Torso*, influenced Michelangelo, whose ideal of physical beauty was powerfully affected by it. Raphael borrowed from still another Roman statue, the *Belvedere Apollo*, at least three times, taking the head as the model for his head of St. Stephen in the *Disputa*, a leg for the study of Adam in the same painting, and the position of the legs for his painting, the *Sistine Madonna*.

Late Renaissance painting is, in fact, full of such borrowings. But the greatest painters and sculptors of the age were primarily interested in expressing their own feelings about God, nature and the beauty of human form, not mimicking the feelings of the ancients. Donatello's sculpture became less classical, not more so, after his sojourn as a "treasure hunter" in Rome, and the figures in Michelangelo's *Last Judgment* defied rigid precepts of classical form. The only truly "classical" statues of the 16th Century were the figures turned out in the hundreds by minor masters for use in gardens and grottoes.

The art of the Renaissance remained, overwhelmingly, religious art. Pagan Rome and Greece challenged the plastic sense, not the spirituality, of the later artists. And their patrons' love for classical books and objects did not deflect them from a preference for art with Christian subject matter. In sculpture pagan subjects were mostly restricted to small bronzes and medals, and in painting they were transformed into allegory. Botticelli's painting of *Pallas Taming the Centaur*—wisdom overcoming a barbarian—symbolized, for 15th Century Florence, the boldness with which their own Lorenzo de' Medici had bested his enemy, the King of Naples, and the wisdom of his peace terms. Moreover, just as the Middle Ages had managed to put a good face on Ovid by allegorizing his message on physical love into the love of man for God, so the Renaissance read into ancient religion and poetry a prefiguring of the truths of Christianity.

One of the few Renaissance artists who, in addition to his other work, did produce some paintings without religious or allegorical significance was Piero di Cosimo. These were scenes from primitive life. But he was a solitary and eccentric man; Vasari says that "he kept himself constantly shut up . . . would not permit anyone to see him work, but lived the life of a wild beast rather than that of a man. He would never suffer his rooms to be swept, and would eat at such moments as he felt hungry . . . he would allow himself no better food than hard-boiled eggs, and to save firing . . . cooked these only when he had prepared a fire to boil his glues, varnishes, etc."

This portrait of the artist as a neurotic is rare for the 15th Century. Although there were a few like Piero—and like Uccello, whom Vasari described as "solitary, strange, melancholy and poor"—artists, generally speaking, did not inhabit private creative worlds. The revolution of Renaissance art could scarcely have taken place if painters, sculptors and architects had not been involved in the changing culture of their day, and they could not have become involved if they had worked in solitude.

At the same time they could not have found the courage to go beyond conventional art if they had not also come to regard themselves less as craftsmen for hire, and more as men of independent genius. The artists of the 14th Century—even famous artists like Giotto—had been members of craft guilds. Working with others in a shop, they had been paid almost by the yard and, like any other craftsmen, were expected to follow directions and deliver the goods. One day it might be a fresco; the next a painted shield; the day after a decorated chest. Some painting shops were more popular than others, just as some jewelers were, but neither the idea nor the word "genius" had been connected with individual workers.

Outside the world of the workshop, however, among scholars and educated men of means, theories were developing about man that were relevant to the role of the artist. During the 15th Century art began to emerge from the anonymity of the workshop. The Renaissance artist was in somewhat the same position as an actor in the 19th Century theater: his profession amused gentlemen, but the same gentlemen would have been outraged to see their children enter it. Michelangelo's father, a city magistrate, tried to beat his son out of his disgraceful desire to become a sculptor. It took the personal intervention of Lorenzo de' Medici to persuade the old man that there was a difference in status between the man who chiseled statues and one who chipped building stones.

The reaction of Michelangelo's father to his son's profession may have been more drastic than most, but it is not difficult to see why he was distressed. Alberti, it is true, came from an aristocratic family, and Brunelleschi and Leonardo were the sons of respectable middle-class notaries. But Uccello's father was a barber, Filippo Lippi's a butcher, Andrea del Castagno's a farmer, and Botticelli's a tanner. The Pollaiuolo family were poultry dealers, Fra Bartolommeo's father a muleteer, and Andrea

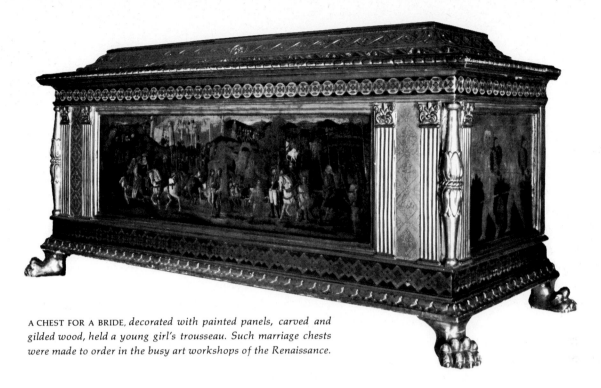

A CHEST FOR A BRIDE, *decorated with painted panels, carved and gilded wood, held a young girl's trousseau. Such marriage chests were made to order in the busy art workshops of the Renaissance.*

del Sarto, as his name suggests, was a tailor's son. Fine company!

Not until the 16th Century—when Raphael, Bramante and Titian lived like princes, and the aged and honored Michelangelo could have done so had he not preferred solitary squalor—did many of the most successful painters make more than a thriving shopkeeper. Some of them lived on an artisan's wage, or less, and none of them had any professional freedom. An artist had to join his guild and observe its rules. In 1434, when Brunelleschi refused to pay his dues to the building workers, the guild to which he belonged, he was arrested and thrown into prison. Only the efforts of the cathedral authorities, for whom he was then working, got him released.

By the 1430s one artist had already tried to lift himself above this menial position by elevating the dignity of his calling. Cennino Cennini, in his *Book on Art*, appealed to his fellow painters to seek social advancement and respect, and detailed for them the steps by which this change could be accomplished: "Your life should always be regulated as if you were studying theology, philosophy or other sciences, that is: eat and drink temperately at least twice a day, consuming light but sustaining food and light wines. There is one more rule which,

if followed, can render your hand so light that it will float, even fly like a leaf in the wind, and that is: not to enjoy too much the company of women."

About this time, too, the classical writings of Pliny and Vitruvius were in circulation, and artists could learn about the lives of their counterparts in ancient Rome—how respected they had been, and what high standards of intellectual attainment had been expected of them. Vitruvius, for example, had demanded as high a level of culture for the architect as Cicero had demanded for the orator. Patterning themselves on these ideals, Renaissance artists became thinkers as well as decorators. And their patrons, whose own increasingly sophisticated needs caused them to single out intellectually gifted men for employment, came to look upon artists as more than craftsmen.

"I have ever striven . . . to examine the ways of nature, to discover how pictures are conceived, how the sense of sight works and in what manner the canons of paintings and sculptures can be determined," wrote Ghiberti in his autobiography. From Cennini onward there was an attempt to associate the practice of painting and sculpture and architecture with the practice of such skills as poetry and mathematics—to represent them as liberal arts, as well as manual ones. And since the disciplines of poetry and mathematics proceeded from a basis of theory, so too should art: "Those who devote themselves to practice without science," wrote Leonardo, "are like sailors who put to sea without rudder or compass and who can never be certain where they are going. Practice must always be founded on sound theory."

By the turn of the 16th Century the battle for status had been won, but an internal war had begun. Painters and sculptors argued over which of them was the more socially acceptable. Leonardo gave the palm to painters because they could work at ease, like gentlemen, while the sculptors, knocking away at the stone with sweat pouring down their faces, worked in conditions like those of a blacksmith.

Also, the moment that painting, sculpture and architecture came to be accepted as gentlemanly professions, their practice became associated with the notion of gentlemanly behavior so persuasively set forth by Castiglione. A gentleman, said Castiglione in his *Courtier*, ought to carry his learning easily and lightly. This notion colors Vasari's opinions about the artists of his day; he placed special emphasis on their speed and dexterity. Indeed, said Vasari, one of the benefits of the technical experiments of the 14th and 15th Centuries was that the skilled painter now had "a degree of perfection which renders it possible for him . . . to produce six pictures in one year, whereas formerly those earlier masters of our art could produce one picture only in six years." Vasari commented on Leonardo's slow rate of production and was proud of his own enormous turnover—he bragged of painting the Great Hall in the Chancellor's Palace in Rome in 100 days flat. ("That's obvious!" sniffed Michelangelo.)

No sculptor, even with a host of assistants, could work this fast. Nor, because of the amount of noise he made, could he work to music, as Leonardo did when he painted the *Mona Lisa*. Chafing under this inferiority, one sculptor, Benvenuto Cellini, pointed out that just as Cicero's ideal orator had to be master of many skills to represent his clients adequately, so a sculptor had to know about war, music and rhetoric in order to portray a soldier, a musician or a statesman. His contemporary and rival, Baccio Bandinelli, tried to disguise his second-class position by calling his sculpture workshop an academy, after the gatherings of learned literary men.

This rivalry within the arts, however much it demeaned individuals, actually advanced the status of the arts as a whole. The process reached a culmination of sorts with the publication, in 1607, of a treatise by the painter Federico Zuccari, placing *disegno* (drawing) just below theology in importance and claiming that *disegno* derived from the phrase *segno di Dio*—a sign from God. Behind the claim lay the idea of genius: the artist, in creating, duplicates one of God's own functions. Leonardo expressed the idea directly; "that divine power, which lies in the knowledge of the painter," he said, "transforms the mind of the painter into the likeness of the divine mind, for with a free hand he can produce different beings, animals, plants, fruits, landscapes, open fields, abysses, terrifying and fearful places."

But the creative element in art, which is nowadays taken for granted, could not be achieved until painters had mastered the technique of reproducing what they actually saw. That done, a good painter, wanting further challenge, sought to alter what was before his eyes and in so doing created something that, until that moment, had not existed. It was at this moment that the artist's similarity to God came to mind, and it is surely no accident that Leonardo was one of the first to whom it occurred. More than any other artist of his time, Leonardo tried to pin down the actions that created form—the beating of a bird's wing, the direction of the currents when a waterfall smashes down into a pool.

Almost as soon as they became creators, artists saw themselves as creatures possessed of divine madness, marked out from other men, heroically doomed to be social outcasts, eccentric and unique. By the middle of the 16th Century there was very little left of the conception of the artist as a more or less anonymous Jack-of-all-crafts. Painters could be given titles of nobility, as Vasari was, and a monarch could stoop to retrieve a fallen brush, as the Emperor Charles V did Titian's. And artists had acquired the prerogative of living beyond convention, a tradition that has ever since appealed to small talents that require the protective coloring of Bohemia.

Early in the 1560s, when Cosimo de' Medici gave his sanction to the formation of an academy of artists that would embrace all the arts, the old guild structure was as good as dead. Artists were no longer workmen. Fanned by the giant pinions of Michelangelo, they were now an elite fraternity headed jointly by Michelangelo and Cosimo himself. The Academy included some of the most illustrious artists of the day: Cellini, Titian, Tintoretto, Salviati—the last of whom, according to Vasari, loved "to mix with men of learning and great persons, and . . . always hated plebeian craftsmen." A gentleman indeed.

Apart from bolstering the status-consciousness of its members—and this is no sneer, for a feeling of proud independence enabled an artist to experiment freely up to the limit of a patron's patience—the Academy achieved little. But it did represent an attitude toward art which encouraged treasuring even a master's preliminary sketches and unfinished statues, like Michelangelo's *Slaves*, as containing sparks of the creative fire. And in 1574 it commemorated Michelangelo's death by erecting a grandiose tomb that combined veneration for the man with praise for the three arts which he had helped to make divine: architecture, painting and sculpture. Architecture is represented by the sarcophagus, sculpture by a bust, and painting by a frescoed canopy which crowns the whole edifice. The tomb is more than a monument to the sculptor of the *David*, the painter of the Sistine Chapel ceiling, and the architect of Florence's Laurentian Library; it is a memorial to the victory of art over craft.

Although almost all the names mentioned so far have been those of Florentines, Florence had no monopoly on talent. In Siena, painters like Duccio di Buoninsegna and the brothers Pietro and Ambrogio Lorenzetti were producing works that ranked in quality with those of their Florentine contemporary, Giotto. But Florence was important in a special way. It had an unusually large number of artists of genius, and the work of these artists created a theme upon which lesser painters could play variations superior in range and intelligence to any they might have created on their own.

Only in one city, Venice, did Florentine painting fail to dominate the local style. Although a number of Florentines worked there—among them Ghiberti, Uccello, Alberti and Andrea del Castagno —they could not deflect the cautious Venetians from their own blend of Byzantine and Gothic styles.

In architecture, too, Venice remained conservative. The intricate and richly encrusted Ca' d'Oro, a *palazzo* on the Grand Canal, was completed at around the same time that Alberti, in Florence, was designing his severely classical Palazzo Rucellai. Venice did not get a classical church until Mauro Coducci built San Michele in Isola, between 1469 and 1479, and the city's first classical *palazzo*, Vendramin, was not begun until about 1481. In Padua, Venice's near neighbor, Andrea

Mantegna was painting cycles of frescoes that showed a passionate concern for antiquity and the new perspective, but the canny Venetian patrons remained uninterested. Like true traders, they were unwilling to buy until the product had proved its worth.

Consequently, even Venetian painters who were familiar with Tuscan work were careful to restrict its influence. Jacopo Bellini experimented with it in his drawings, but his paintings remained bright and pretty and made no new intellectual demands on their viewers. Not until the career of Jacopo's son, Giovanni, did Venice get a painter who dared to use the advanced techniques of Florence—and Giovanni accomplished this by painting in a gentle and devout manner. From this beginning Florentine techniques gradually merged with the three qualities in which Venetians had always excelled—glowing color, splendor of subject, and psychological penetration. But the merger did not reach maturity until the 16th Century, with the works of Giorgione, Veronese and Titian.

Soon after 1500 leadership in art passed from Florence to Rome. The prestige of the papal court, and its enormous architectural projects, such as the rebuilding of St. Peter's, attracted artists of the stature of Raphael and Michelangelo and architects like the great Bramante of Milan. Although some painters, like the Florentines Fra Bartolommeo and Andrea del Sarto, carried on the native artistic traditions by working primarily in their home city, the greatest opportunities and the liveliest competition were now to be found in Rome. Rome also offered, in Pope Julius II, one of the most intelligent and forceful art patrons the world has ever known. Julius cared about both theology and antiquity, and the commissions he offered set his artists fierce challenges.

The career of one artist, Raphael, shows how styles changed in the Vatican's air. Raphael had begun his career by leaving his birthplace, Urbino, to paint with Perugino. He took on his master's manner: gentle, unpretentious, but with a remarkably shrewd grasp of perspective. Then a stay in Florence opened his eyes to the monumental strength of Masaccio, and the genius of his elders, Leonardo and Michelangelo. Ultimately, he emerged as a portraitist of serene but incisive power and a draftsman of astonishing virtuosity, with a line that could be a mere blandishment or as incisive as a whiplash.

By 1509, aged 26, Raphael had arrived in Rome and was working for Julius. First he did the frescoes in the room called the Stanza della Segnatura in the Vatican. The theme, or program, for the frescoes was probably drawn up for the Pope by his humanist advisers, and was extremely complicated. But Raphael succeeded in producing a cycle of paintings which has variously been called the pictorial encyclopedia of humanism and the apotheosis of the classical style. Certainly if any one painting had to be singled out to exemplify the technical accomplishment and intellectual assurance of the finest Renaissance art, the *School of Athens* fresco from this room would almost inevitably be the choice.

The theme of the *School of Athens* is the reconciliation of the two most important humanist philosophies, Plato's and Aristotle's, one mystical, the other practical. This painting has its theological counterpart in the fresco on the opposite wall, the *Dispute on the Nature of the Sacrament*. The frescoes on the other two walls represent the two other principal fields of human achievement: poetry and law. Conceived as an essay on Intellect, the four end up as proof of the ascendancy of Art.

When the first Stanza was completed, Raphael was given a second one—subsequently called the Stanza d'Eliodoro—to decorate. Its program, too,

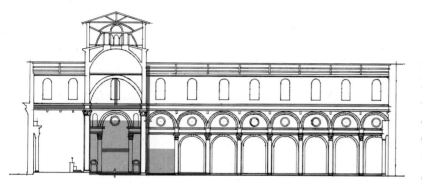

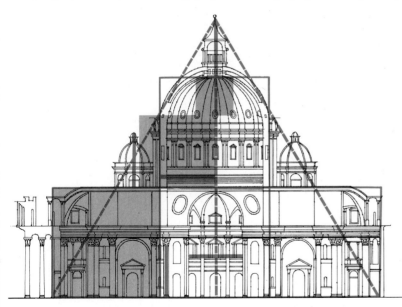

HARMONIOUS PROPORTIONS *preoccupied Renaissance architects, who tried to relate the dimensions of every major part of their buildings to one module, or basic unit of length. In Brunelleschi's church of San Lorenzo in Florence (above) the module is one side of the large shaded square. This is twice the width of the side aisles (small square) and one half the height of the building (below the roof line). Michelangelo, a century later, used more complex ratios. In his plan for St. Peter's (below), which was never adopted, he used a single module (blue bars) for the width of the crossing (center) and the height of columns, lantern and cupolas. The building's units, measured vertically, are related in a 3:2:1 ratio, as indicated by the shaded areas, the largest unit having a side two modules long. The outline of the building defines an equilateral triangle, a geometric shape perfect in its symmetry.*

was allegorical. Unlike the frescoes in the first, however, these were not to be imaginary assemblies of great men but paintings of actual historical incidents whose allegorical references were to current Church events. Thus the significance of the victory of Pope Julius' army over the powerful army of the French was memorialized in a painting of an event that was thought to have taken place a thousand years before: Pope Leo I miraculously halting the march on Rome of Attila and his invading Huns.

In the second Stanza, where the subjects are not set pieces but scenes of action, Raphael's style takes on a sweep and perturbation suitable to their dramatic content. There is a sharp contrast between the grave, still treatment of the "good" characters and the rushing lines and anatomical exaggerations of the "bad." It is the beginning vocabulary of Mannerism, the restless, artificial style that marked the end of Renaissance painting. By the time Raphael died, in 1520, the style was there to be seen. His last painting, the *Transfiguration*, is full of the spiraling shapes, the hectic gestures and the perfervid intensity of mature Mannerism. Compared to his gentle madonnas it is a whirlwind. Raphael was only 37 when he died (of "too many women," said one sour contemporary), but he probably produced more great works of art, in more styles, than any other painter in history.

But the last of Raphael's styles, Mannerism, was not really his invention. As early as 1502 the Florentine painter Filippino Lippi showed signs of impatience with harmonious, rational art. (Filippino was the son of the better-known Fra Filippo Lippi, the painter-monk who abducted and married a nun.) In the church of Santa Maria Novella in Florence there is a fresco by Filippino that has many of the marks of the Mannerist style. Its treatment is as bizarre as its subject: St. Philip's

127

part in the inadvertent death of a pagan king's son. According to the legend, Philip called forth a ravening monster from the temple of Mars in order to destroy it; as it emerged from its lair the monster overwhelmed the king's son with its horrible smell.

Like Raphael in his *School of Athens*, Filippino uses a classical architectural perspective for the background of St. Philip. Unlike Raphael, he uses it to create not a lucid, idealized setting, but a strangely agitated one, restless and nightmarish. Trophies and vases jab the air with abrupt accents. The ruins he pictures, instead of being dignified and archeologically convincing, express a fanciful unease.

The revolt against rational art quickened in 1516 when the Florentine painter Giovanni Rosso dared to play visual tricks with reality. Rosso produced a fresco for the Church of the Annunziata in Florence in which one of the figures is shown with his robe spilling over the picture's border. Thereafter Rosso, his Florentine contemporary, Jacopo da Pontormo, and two other painters —Domenico Beccafumi in Siena and Francesco Parmigianino in Parma—turned their backs on the classical style to paint in a style that was subjective and irrational.

The reasons for their revolt were partly sociological. Like the earlier painters who had retreated from Giotto's realism to medieval symbolism under the pressure of distressful events—mostly the plague—the Mannerist painters were also retreating from events in the external world. Fear and unrest made an orderly, harmonious art seem incompatible. For the Mannerists the cause was not disease, but the series of French and Spanish invasions, the defeats and constitutional crises that swept over the Italian peninsula starting late in the 15th Century.

Of course sociology alone cannot explain Mannerism. For one thing it was never a uniform style, and therefore cannot have had entirely external causes. Some of Mannerism sprang from changes in the individual artist. In learning to be independent, he learned to be conscious of himself as a person; he was revolting against a style that seemed to leave him nothing to explore. Having given the world one standard by which to judge art, the classical, Italy now gave it another, the anticlassical. Between these two poles, objective and subjective, all subsequent art has swung and all art criticism wavered.

Was this 200 years of experiment and change welcomed by the society that spawned it? Or was the artist considered an inspired crank? Apparently, the former. Giotto was popular not merely with the small clique of farsighted men who hired him, but presumably with the vast congregations who passed through the churches he painted. Donatello's *Judith and Holofernes*, Michelangelo's *David* and Cellini's *Perseus* were all revolutionary and all were set up for the public gaze in the most prickly and critical city in Italy, but there are scarcely any stories of the daubing or mutilation of statues in Renaissance times.

Was this perhaps because men were indifferent to art? Or was it because they wanted an art which celebrated the real world, not eternity, and one that arose from the circumstances of ordinary life, not mystical vision?

Surely the latter. Although there are astonishingly few records of a personal response to art until the 16th Century, almost no books or letters expressing individual likes or dislikes, there is plenty of evidence of a lively community interest in the building of churches and the unveiling of statues. In a sense Renaissance art, by breaking with tradition, was part of the process of man's liberation from medieval conformity, a straitjacket from which he had been longing to escape.

A SELF-PORTRAIT *in chalk shows Leonardo da Vinci (1452-1519) toward the end of his life.*

THE SCOPE OF GENIUS

Leonardo da Vinci personified the Renaissance spirit: he explored everything and excelled in nearly all his ventures. He was so busy in so many areas that though he was one of the greatest artists of the age he had little time to paint; he died having finished few pictures. His curiosity about nature led him deep into anatomy, botany, geology, mechanics and astronomy. In more than 5,000 pages of notes, he drew up plans that anticipated such inventions as the helicopter, the submarine, the machine gun and the automobile. In one collection of his works, he proudly signed his name, "Leonardo da Vinci, disciple of experiment."

An artist's penetrating analysis of the human body

Hands, accenting bone and muscle structure.

Leonardo was a pioneer anatomist who sought to render with exquisite draughtsmanship his detailed knowledge of the human body. Almost every Renaissance artist made studies of hands—however, Leonardo based his sketches *(left)* on observations of bones, muscles, nerves and veins. This attention to detail also led him to formulate ideal proportions for drawing figures, as shown by the lines dividing the face below. Gross deformities intrigued him as much as beauty; according to one account, he once got a band of peasants drunk so he could sketch the sodden bestiality of their faces. His caricatures of old men *(opposite, below)* reflect a searching interest in the grotesque expressions of age.

Internal structure and outward form had an equal fascination for Leonardo. In one set of drawings, he demonstrated how the eye works *(opposite, top)*, showing that light rays enter the pupil and project an image on the retina. Investigating the body, Leonardo produced the most beautiful and accurate anatomical studies of his day *(right)*. He gained precise knowledge by dissecting more than 30 cadavers—until at last Pope Leo X barred him from the mortuary in Rome.

A man's face, scaled to ideal proportions.

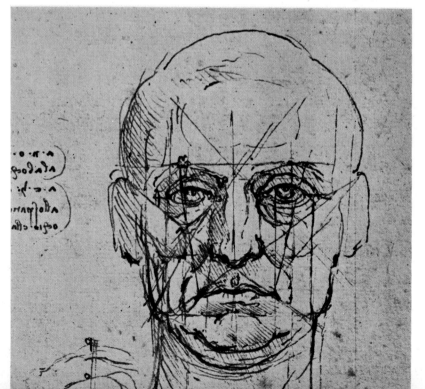

The human eye depicted in outward form.

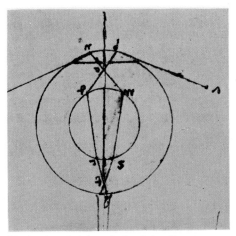
Mechanics of vision shown in a diagram.

Skeletal studies made from actual dissections.

Aged faces, drawn about 1490, reflecting the temperaments of man.

A painstaking study of the myriad forms of life

Branching patterns of two trees.

Plants and animals intrigued Leonardo as much as the human figure. His wide-ranging eye encompassed the full spectrum of life, from the movements of a crab or a cat to the growth patterns of a flower or a tree. At first he made his drawings of plants as studies for paintings. But gradually he grew interested in botany for its own sake. He noted before other observers that various types of trees branch in their own distinct patterns *(left)*. With a botanist's eye for detail he sketched individual limbs *(below, left)*, measuring changes in the girth of a single stem as it spreads.

The studies of a horse's foreleg on the opposite page enabled Leonardo to draw the realistic horse pictured above it. The analysis of structural similarities between the legs of horses and humans, shown opposite, was one of the first known studies in the field of comparative anatomy.

Madonna lily, a preliminary sketch for a painting.

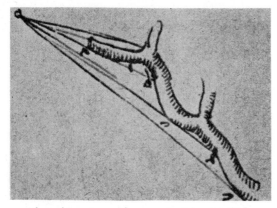

A branching stem with segments of varying thickness.

A quince bloom, from a study of buds and unfolding flowers.

Crabs, drawn crawling and curled.

Feline poses, a study made for a treatise on the movement of animals.

Prancing horse, a sketch of an equestrian statue for the Duke of Milan.

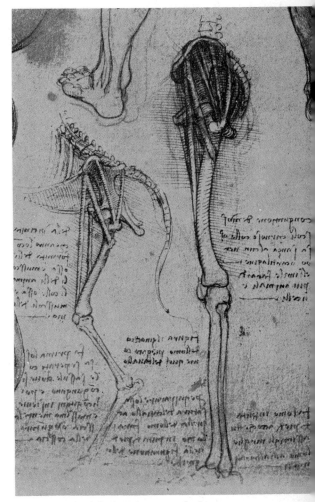

Bone structure of the leg of a man and a horse.

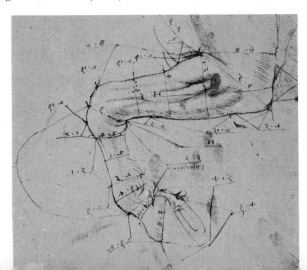

Foreleg of a horse, measured to exact proportions.

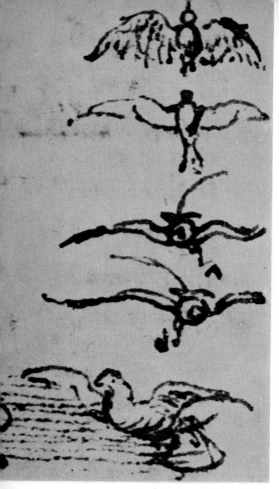

Wingspreads of birds in flight.

Ingenious designs
to put man in the air

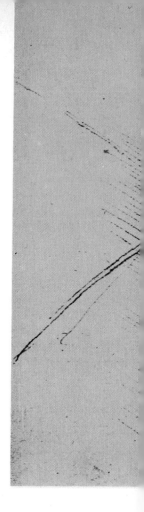

Many men of the Renaissance dreamed of flying; a few even jumped off towers in exotic winged contraptions. Leonardo shared the dream and designed many flying machines, confident that someday one would work and "fill the world with its great fame." He spent years observing birds in flight *(left)*. He studied and sketched the machinery he would need—for example, a block and tackle *(opposite, right)* to test the tension of ropes, or a hand crank *(opposite, bottom)*. One of his early flying machines *(below)* used a similar crank to operate batlike wings. A later refinement *(right)* used stirrups and pulleys, so that a flier could flap the wings with his legs.

No one knows if Leonardo ever really got aloft, but one contemporary left a pretty good clue. "Leonardo da Vinci also tried to fly, but he, too, failed," he said—adding as a wry afterthought, "He was a magnificent painter."

A wooden wing hooked up to a hand crank.

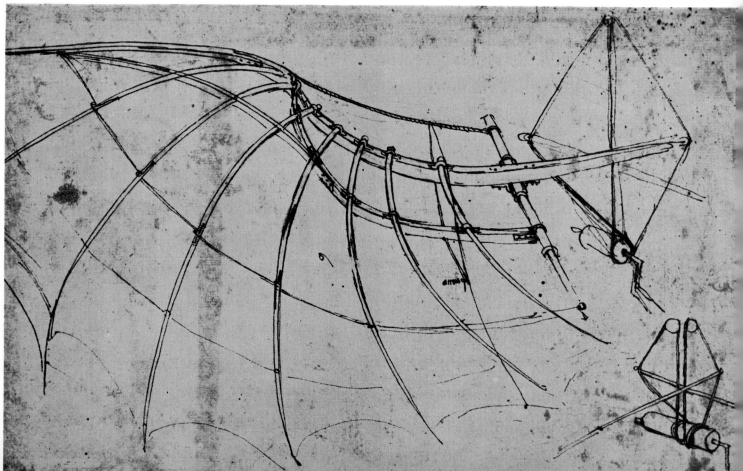

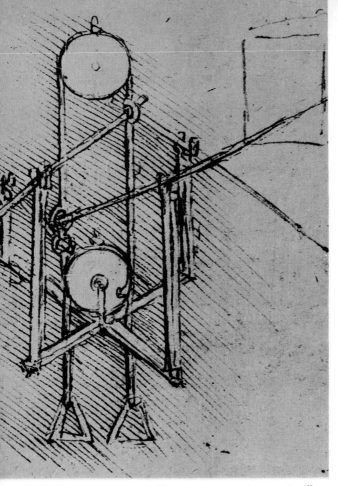

Stirrups pulling ropes over a system of pulleys.

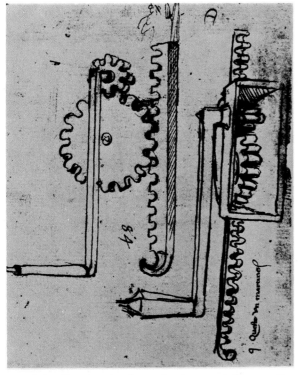

Crank for changing circular motion to up-and-down motion.

Tackle (right) for studying tension exerted on ropes.

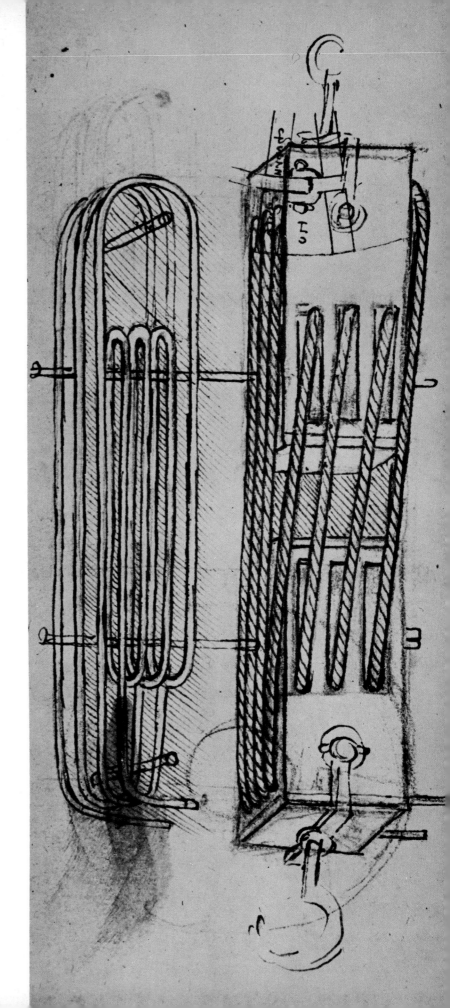

An aerial view of the rivers and land in the Arezzo province.

A test for mirrors, drawn to show the path of light rays.

Leonardo's experiments and studies constantly shifted between the functional and the theoretical. For example, his topographical maps *(above)* were the basis of practical plans to prevent floods and to aid irrigation. His ventures in astronomy, on the other hand, could be highly abstract. On a page from his notebook crowded with imposing calculations and diagrams, shown opposite, he established the relative sizes of the sun and the moon—and was totally wrong.

Often, though, theory and practice went hand in hand. In optics, he correctly observed that a light's intensity varies in direct proportion to its distance from a light source *(opposite, top)*. He also worked out a test for the quality of mirrors, similar to one still in use, based on the reflection of light rays *(right)*. And he devised the first telescope—his "glasses to see the moon magnified" —with which he could see and sketch the moon in an eclipse *(center)*. He worked on every problem he could think of with the same unlimited exuberance. In this, he expressed the original, vital spirit of his age.

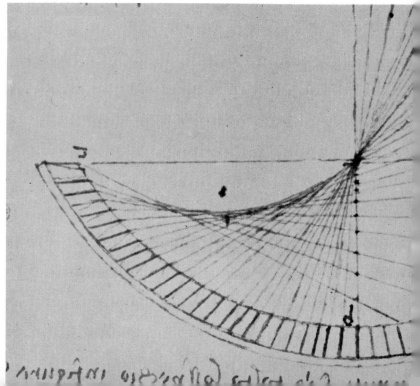

136

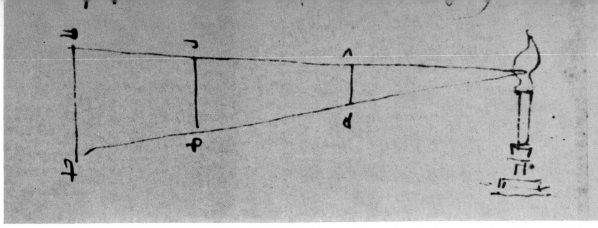

Candlelight, a study showing the change of its intensity over a distance.

The sun and moon, with their sizes exhaustively calculated.

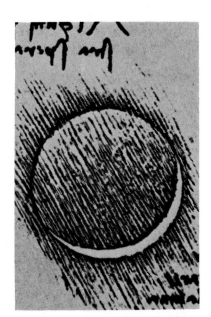

The moon, approaching total eclipse.

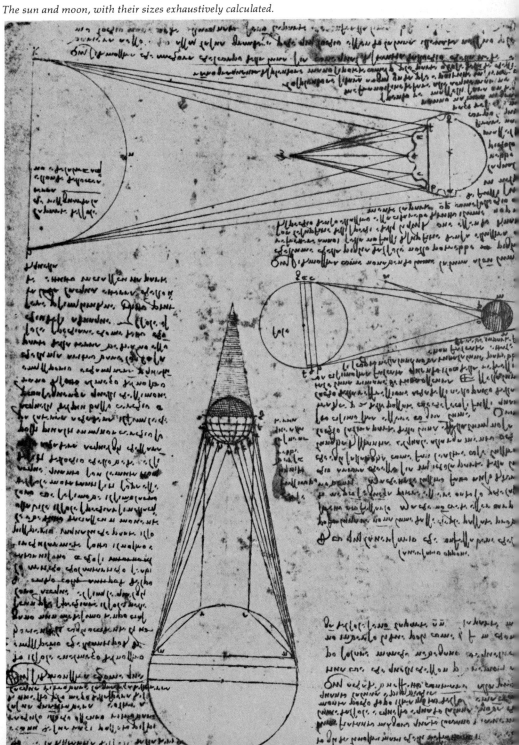

7

WAR AND POLITICS

FLORENTINE HORSEMEN *with armor, imposing helmets and lances fight in this 1432 battle against Siena depicted by Uccello. For all their knightly dress, most Renaissance soldiers were mercenaries, many of them ill paid.*

Although historians are generally reluctant to look upon any one year as constituting a dramatic turning point in the fortunes of a people, many a nation does look back—as France looks back to 1789 and the United States to 1776—to a single event that came down like a chopper on the threads of national development.

For Italians of the late Renaissance the year was 1494; the event was the invasion of a French army under King Charles VIII. For the next two generations Italy was a battlefield, and when the smoke cleared and the blood had been stanched, it was felt that, except for here and there in the arts, the peninsula's glory had departed. Italian armies had been trounced by Frenchmen, Spaniards, Germans and Swiss. City after city had been stormed. Rome itself had been sacked. The closed and tranquil world of the 15th Century had been broken into, the treasure house looted, the proud, refined voice of Italian freedom shouted down by orders barked from beyond the Alps and over the sea. Licking the wounds to their pride and prosperity, Italians looked back on the summer of 1494—to a time just before the French had come down into Lombardy in September—as the season that closed their golden age.

Contemporary historians were unanimous in pronouncing 1494 as a year of desolation. Before it, wrote Corio, the historian of Milan, "everyone believed that peace had come to stay; everyone was intent on getting rich, and all paths were open to them. Feasting and entertainments held the field; the world seemed more stable than ever before."

Francesco Guicciardini referred to "those happy times before '94" in his *History of Florence* (1509). A generation later, during which he had seen matters go from bad to worse, Guicciardini expanded this wistful reference to better times into bitter threnody. In his *History of Italy* (1536-1540) he wrote: "The calamities of Italy began . . . to the greater sorrow and terror of all men, at a time when circumstances seemed universally most propitious and fortunate. . . . Italy had never known such prosperity, or such a desirable condition as that which it enjoyed in all tranquillity in the year of Our Lord 1490 and the years immediately before and after."

These examples could be multiplied. For the historians of individual cities, and of Italy as a whole, 1494 was "that most unhappy year." Only in Venice, whose humiliation was not to come until 1509, could men look back on 1494 without a jolt of anguish.

Why was the French invasion so catastrophic? What brought it about? And what were its consequences?

It was not just that French troops swung down into Lombardy, frightened Florence and the Pope into supporting their promenade southward, made their way as conquerors into Naples, left garrisons there and marched back up the peninsula, and went home a year later. All this, while sensational enough, and deeply humiliating to the Italians, was not in itself a catastrophe. After all, Italy had been invaded before. Most Italian observers, though they were deeply disturbed by the events of 1494-1495, thought that the danger had passed with the departure of the French; with the fatalism that an act of God might have produced, they went once more about their business. But they were wrong. In 1499 the French invaded Lombardy again. In 1500 the new French King, Louis XII, and the Spanish monarch, Ferdinand of Aragon, agreed to split up the Kingdom of Naples between them, and the armies of both countries began operations there in 1501.

In this double occupation lay the real catastrophe, for in 1502 the invaders fell out between themselves. From that moment Italy was doomed to be the arena in which the two most potent and aggressive powers in Europe tried their strength. Another French army was dispatched. This was resoundingly defeated at the River Garigliano in 1503 by the Spaniards under Gonzalo de Córdoba, known in his own day, and since, as the Great Captain. Louis was forced to consider coming to terms with Ferdinand, but when the two reached an agreement, it was not to leave poor Italy alone, but to involve themselves more closely with her affairs, to conquer Venice with the aid of Maximilian of Hapsburg, and, later, to reduce the pope to a Franco-Spanish puppet.

There was much here that was irrational. France was a wealthy and self-supporting country. No need lay behind her desire for conquest in Italy. The obvious route for French expansion, moreover, was not over the Alps and into Italy with its long, thin, difficult-to-guard lines of communications, but northeast, across an easy plain into the Netherlands. Brussels and Antwerp were the logical economic targets, not Venice, inaccessible in her lagoons, or Naples, rich in grain which France in any case did not need. In the same way it was not need or economic advantage that sent Spanish armies to Italy. In spite of the growing administrative unity of the European powers, in spite of the sophistication of their bureaucracies and fiscal policies and legal reforms, their foreign policy was still primitive, motivated less by reason than by greed, by a thirst for glory and sheer adventurousness.

Real motives aside, there were plenty of high-sounding excuses, though of questionable legality, for the French invasions. Charles VIII had inherited the Angevin claim to the throne of Naples, and he announced his intention of enforcing it. But he would never have marched south if he had not, as a sickly child, been reared on a heady diet of chivalrous romances, and if he had not seen himself as the glorious leader of a crusade against the Turks, using southern Italy as a base.

There was nothing reasonable about this. There was nothing reasonable about the way in which he bought the neutrality of Spain and Germany by giving away territories in southern and eastern France which had been painfully acquired by his father. But the element of unreason was, in fact, a strength when it came to dealing with the Italian courts. Italian diplomats had been schooled in their own cautious and businesslike world to see foreign policy in rational terms: they were nonplused by the essentially irrational behavior of the feudal dynasts of the north.

Italian diplomacy, technically so advanced, was at fault in two other ways. Lulled by the comparative tranquillity of the years since the middle of the 15th Century into thinking that shrewd diplomacy could prevent wars, the Italian states and their ambassadors believed clever negotiations would dissuade France and Spain from carving up Italy. "Before our Italian princes were scourged by the foreigners," wrote Machiavelli in 1522, "they thought it enough for princes to write a handsome letter, or return a pointed answer." The second fault was a failure on the part of diplomatic envoys abroad to see past the gossip and personalities of the court to the realities that affected a nation's desire and capacity to go to war: the frame of mind of its nobility, the number of men available to fight, and the country's financial resources.

These failings, plus a certain fastidiousness that made it difficult at first for Italians to take the "barbarians" wholly seriously, plus again a reluctance on the part of the Italian states to pay enough heed to the warnings of their diplomats abroad, all helped Italians to see each invasion as the last. As a result they did not adopt the necessary, if painfully novel, solution: firm alliances to repel would-be invaders.

We are so used to the idea of a united Italy that it is difficult not to feel some exasperation at this failure of the Italian states to ward off aggression —as they could have done so easily, from a military point of view—by putting up a coordinated opposition. But Italy was a land that contained a large number of independent states, just as Europe itself did, and we must not be misled by the common tongue and the shared pride in descent from ancient Rome into thinking that the separate states of Italy were any more prepared to link their fortunes—save for immediate self-interest—than were France and Germany or Spain and Portugal.

There *were* leagues of Italian states: the papacy combined with Venice, Milan and others to oppose the retreating French army in 1495, for instance. But such leagues were composed to meet one particular emergency, and were then dissolved. And not all such leagues were aimed against the foreigner: in 1509 the papacy, Ferrara and Mantua joined the Holy Roman Empire, France and Spain in their attack on Venice. All of them assumed, falsely, that their violent visitors had not come to stay, and each Italian state offered aid—troops, unhindered communications, provender—in order to gain support for its own local squabbles.

It is quite likely that even if foreign invasion had not come, the last years of the 15th Century would have seen the outbreak of wars in Italy. Although the 1454 Peace of Lodi, which settled disputes between most of the Italian states, lasted an uneasy 40 years, this was because the three principals—Venice, Florence and Milan—were reasonably content with the frontiers they obtained by this settlement and required time to consolidate them. The Peace of Lodi could not conceal forever that Milan and Venice were doomed by geography to be uneasy neighbors, as were Naples and the papacy. Milan and Naples, whose spheres of influence in no way overlapped, tended to support each other diplomatically, and it was with this axis that Florence cautiously aligned herself—partly because Venice was the weightiest possible aggressor state and the most direct rival to Florentine trade overseas, and partly because any strengthening of control by the papacy over its territories east of the Apennines was a threat to the Florentine frontier there.

Guicciardini described Lorenzo de' Medici as "applying a sort of balance" to the Italian political scene, and many later historians have seen the post-Lodi period as a trial run, on a small scale, for the balance-of-power principle which consciously motivated the European alliances of the succeeding centuries. But this is most unlikely. Diplomacy in 15th Century Italy was based on expediency. What looks, in retrospect, like the conscious application of the principle of balance of power was merely a series of decisions based on immediate necessity. The existence of marriage ties and trading links with France and Spain, the existence of historical links with the Empire and the importance of trade routes across the Alps meant that Italy was not a closed political system. The need to placate or to curry favor with other powers sentenced the rulers of Italy to conduct their long-term political plans always with an eye to forces outside the peninsula.

Much depended on personalities. The death of Lorenzo the Magnificent in 1492 meant that Italy had lost one guarantee of moderation, for his son Piero was a comparatively dim and fickle personality. Then the election of Rodrigo Borgia as Pope Alexander VI in the same year brought to the leadership of the Papal States a man more aggressive and even less scrupulous than Sixtus. Both these events came at a time when Lodovico Sforza was becoming increasingly nervous regarding his own position in Milan. He was its effective ruler, but the legitimate head of the state was his nephew, Gian Galeazzo Sforza, and Gian Galeazzo's wife was constantly urging her father, the King of Naples, to support her husband's claim to actual rule. This tension within the Milan-Naples axis was increased by Lodovico's doubts of Piero's support, and he turned instead to the King of France, promising to support Charles if he would enter Italy and assert the Angevin claim to Naples.

Such appeals from Italian princes to foreign monarchs had been made before. Commonly it had been a matter of bluff. It was Italy's misfortune that this time France, wholly recovered from the dislocations of the Hundred Years' War, and with a restless and militant nobility, actually came.

In the same way it was unfortunate for Italy that Spain was at this point able to take a more active interest in Italian affairs. Firmly governed by her joint monarchs, Isabella of Castile and Ferdinand of Aragon, Spain had concluded her centuries-long crusade against the Moors by defeating the last infidel state, Granada, in 1492. Now she had a large army which had nothing to do; she was also better administered than she had ever been before. As a result, she was able to involve herself in Italy—sometimes in league with France, as in those early days in Naples and in the general onslaught on Venice in 1509, but eventually in ferocious rivalry with her.

The details of the Italian wars—where the great European beasts mauled one another and the Italian jackal states danced round excitedly picking up the fragments of their prey—are too complex to be followed here. Indeed, since Guicciardini's *History of Italy* no historian has had the stomach to deal fully with them. But it is worth taking a look at some of their results.

When Guicciardini died in 1540, Milan and Naples were Spanish possessions and the historian's own Florence was neither free nor independent; her republican constitution was replaced by hereditary princely rule, and her fortresses were held by a representative of the Emperor Charles V. Rome and the Pope remained, but only 13 years earlier the city had been pillaged by Spanish and German troops and the Pope held for ransom. Venice had in 1509 been cut back to her lagoons by the greatest military defeat in her history, and her mainland possessions were divided among France, Germany

A FANCIFUL WARSHIP, *this naval fortress was designed by Robertus Valturius, an artist who worked for the tyrant Sigismondo Malatesta. Many artists doubled as military engineers: Leonardo da Vinci, for example, designed armaments for the Duke of Milan; Michelangelo for the magistrates of Florence.*

and the papacy. The French had captured all or part of the Duchy of Milan four separate times over a period of 25 years before being driven out for good in 1525.

In all this the Italians were not exactly the hopeless victims of fate. Lodovico Sforza had invited the French in in 1494. Sixteen years later Pope Julius II invited the Spaniards in to help drive out the French. The business communities in Milan and Genoa saw the advantages to be gained from a connection with Spain, where Italian bankers already had large investments and were keeping an eye on the growing wealth arriving in Spain from the New World; and this tipped the balance of Italian support against France. There is little doubt that Italian economic life—in the spheres at least of overseas trade and banking—gained from an acceptance of Spanish influence. Constitutional stability and profit seemed a fair exchange for the loss of self-government.

The disasters which began to overcome Italy in 1494 were therefore not absolute. Genoa boomed steadily throughout the following century; Venice remained as strong and prosperous—and as un-Italian—as ever. Florence lived a settled and secure life under her Grand Dukes, even if they had been foisted on her by Spanish pikes. The papacy, which had taken advantage of the general confusion to recapture long-lost cities and to subject the Papal States as a whole to a reasonably efficient administration, was able to rally Catholic Europe into a Counter Reformation and deliver Rome from the shoddy image the Church had cast since the 14th Century. Naples, while heavily taxed by Spain for wars fought by the Emperor in Africa and Hungary and Germany which did not benefit her, was nevertheless freed from the interminable feudal quarrels and petty revolts which had been her theme song in the previous century.

The smaller states, like Mantua and Ferrara,

remained independent, though henceforward they could not expect to extend their borders. The smallest ones of all, places like Imola, Forlì, Faenza and Rimini, were at least freed by subjection to the papacy from the riots and bloodshed that they had known under their often transient tyrant rulers.

As a result of the Treaty of Cambrai in 1529, by which France gave up her claims in Italy, and thanks to the reimposition of Medici rule in Florence in the following year, the peninsula was more settled than it had been since the Roman Empire. Only one trouble spot remained, Siena, over which French and Spanish troops continued to fight until 1557, when it was made over to Cosimo I, Grand Duke of Tuscany, by the King of Spain, Philip II. But all around this tiny volcano, and from 1557 all over Italy, there reigned a wholly uncharacteristic peace.

Anyone who tries to strike a balance and estimate how much Italy had lost or gained at the end of her period of disaster, is bound to take a reasonably optimistic view. For, unless she had been forced into contact with the Atlantic powers, it is likely that she would have suffered economically more than she did. The center of trade, like the center of governmental experiment and cultural advance, was shifting west and north as overseas expansion came to foster the power of Spain, France and the Low Countries. If Italy looks less interesting in the second half of the 16th than in the second half of the 15th Century it is because other states had the task of becoming civilized, settled, expansionist nations still before them. Political stability may be dull, but it is safe.

In the world of the intellect the picture is mixed. The inhibiting effects of resurgent Catholicism are undeniable; the prosecution of the scientist Galileo because his findings conflicted with Church dogma is a sordid example. And just as Giotto had been followed by a host of mere imitators, and

Petrarch by a century of uncreative Ciceronians, the bursts of creativity in the arts and in literature between 1420 and 1500 could be expected to be followed by a period in which imitation was more prominent than advance.

However, this did not prevent Michelangelo from becoming a greater and greater artist all during the time the so-called disasters were going on. Nor did their aftermath prevent Buontalenti from showing his genius as an architect. This is a theme which will arise again in the last chapter; at this point it must suffice to suggest that if the names of men of genius are fewer in the second than in the first half of the 16th Century, it is because there were fewer of them about and there was no longer the ferment of thought which can draw original ideas from secondary talents. The political disasters had nothing to do with that. Paintings continued to be commissioned, churches and palaces built. The career of Caravaggio, who was violent and truculent as an individual and highly unconventional as an artist, shows that genius could make itself heard in 1600 as it had in 1500.

So there is a bright side to look on. That we must look hard to see it is a wry tribute to the abilities of Florentine writers, especially to the historians among them who have held the ear of posterity ever since with their bitterly told tale of woe. For it was in Florence that the sense of disaster was felt most keenly in the first half of the 16th Century. Strongly committed as most of the intellectuals were to some form of republican government, they were desolated to find themselves forced twice by foreign arms to accept—the second time for good—the rule of a family they had earlier expelled. They saw the collapse of a way of life which was consecrated by Roman example, by the triumphs of their medieval past and by their own passionate involvement. Florence entered the wars as the nearest thing to a modern democracy that could then be found in Europe and emerged from them a conventional 16th Century princely state. In contrast, Venice remained a republic. Milan had a foreign governor—but the Sforzas themselves had not been Milanese, and the newcomer hardly modified the functions of her previous princes.

It was in Florence, too, that there existed the strongest sense of affinity with the virtues of courage and faithfulness that had brought such dazzling conquests to the armies of republican Rome. This, coupled with a political puritanism which could accept the amoralism with which a state could switch sides but shrink from personal treachery or coat-turning, made Florentines, of all the Italians, the most bitterly conscious of the moral failings that opened Italy so freely to the once despised barbarians. Guicciardini, the greatest of Florentine historians, came to the conclusion that, although the political and military ineptitude of the Italians had contributed to the humiliating ease with which Charles VIII had marched down the peninsula to Naples, plain weakness of character had also played a large part.

There is an element of masochism in the zeal with which writers like Guicciardini traced their defeats to defects of morale. And it led them perversely to exaggerate the military inefficiency of the Italians. Both he and Machiavelli stressed their unreadiness for the sort of warfare they now had to cope with. They claimed that the Italians were not only psychologically unprepared for battles fought desperately and bloodily, but that they had also been left technically behind by the tactics and equipment (especially artillery) of the French and their Swiss allies.

Machiavelli started from the contention that the Italian armies of his own day were despicable. He explained this by citing the dependence of the Italian cities on hired mercenaries, on men who constituted an unofficial trade union, who were accustomed to playing the game of war according to rules, and who naturally killed as few of one another as possible. By faking the casualties in 15th Century battles down to a few unfortunates who fell off their horses and were suffocated in the mud, Machiavelli created a myth that was to have a long life: of chessboard wars, where gorgeously caparisoned horsemen moved about the battlefield with stately deliberation. If they were removed from the board, it was only for the rest of the game; after a period of honorable captivity, and the payment of a ransom, they were able to return for the next bout.

This distorted view of earlier wars was a result of Machiavelli's special pleading for citizen armies on the Roman model. To push the system he wanted, he had to denigrate the one that preceded it. In reality the professional soldier of Italy in 1494 was as well trained and equipped as his ultramontane adversary. Nor was his personal valor less. In a tourney staged during a lull in the fighting in southern Italy in 1503, thirteen Italian knights fought thirteen Frenchmen and defeated them easily.

Milan had long been exporting armor to the rest of Europe. Her swords and lances and crossbows were as good as those used elsewhere. In the 16th Century, whenever the origin of gunpowder was discussed, it was believed all over Europe that the handgun, precursor of the musket, had been first used in the war between the Venetians and the Genoese in 1378-1381. Fifteenth Century inventories of fortress stores show that Italian castles were reasonably well furnished with cannon. The use of artillery in siege work was a commonplace. Where the French were definitely in the lead was in the use of light artillery, mounted on wheeled carriages, in the field. But in this period guns seldom, if ever, made the difference between victory and defeat in battle.

Somewhat better is the argument that Italian

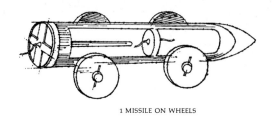

1 MISSILE ON WHEELS

infantry tactics were at fault because they were not based on the pike—a kind of heavy spear carried by foot soldiers. The massed column of pikemen was the characteristic formation of the Swiss, and its tanklike effect won battle after battle for their employers, the French (whose own national army was comprised mainly of cavalry and crossbowmen) until the Spaniards and Italians learned to copy it. The Swiss fought in compact squares of about 6,000 men: 85 shoulder to shoulder, on a 100-yard-long front, and some 70 ranks deep. In defense the pike phalanx presented a bristling hedge of steel, for the pikes were so long that the points of the front four ranks glittered together in the eyes of any horseman bold enough to charge them. In attack, such a column, rumbling forward at a fast walk, had a momentum that only a similar mass could resist.

But the Italians learned quickly, even adopting longer pikes that would spear enemy pikemen first. And while their infantry bands were small and less disciplined than their foes' (and discipline was the essence of such a formation), they nevertheless did hire German Landsknechte to counter the Swiss. Therefore, the pike cannot be brought forward, any more than field artillery, to explain Italy's helplessness at the hands of foreign armies. And it must always be borne in mind that the wars—with only one or two exceptions—did not consist of direct confrontations between exclusively Italian and exclusively foreign armies.

One last technical excuse was made by contemporaries. This was that their fortifications were out-of-date, leaving Italian cities vulnerable to French cannon. But this claim bears examination no better than the others. The introduction of effective siege cannon had necessitated a new form of fortification, with thicker walls, and with bastions at the angles instead of the traditional towers which were vulnerable to the pounding of cannon balls

and too weak to provide platforms for heavy guns. So the towers were modified, experiment by experiment, into the bastions—solid angled triangles, level with the walls—which became the characteristic feature of 16th Century forts all over Europe and wherever Europeans settled overseas.

This development actually had been pioneered by Italian military engineers before the wars began, at sites like Ostia (1482-1486), Brolio (1484) and Poggio Imperiale, where the magnificent (and still standing) fortifications were begun on the orders of Lorenzo the Magnificent in 1487. In the second half of the 16th Century, Italian military engineers were in demand all over Europe. They were employed by Queen Elizabeth in England; they fortified cities in France and Belgium and Hungary. Military engineering was Italy's greatest concealed export in the 16th Century—and the foundations of its expertise had been worked out before the French first broke across the Alps.

Nowhere else was the art of fortification held in such repute. No division was made in Italy between the dignity of civil and ecclesiastical architecture on the one hand and military architecture on the other. Giotto designed the third circuit of the walls of Florence. Brunelleschi designed fortifications at Pisa. Leonardo da Vinci was appointed inspector of fortifications in the Romagna by Cesare Borgia. Michelangelo was put in charge of the fortifications of Florence during the Imperialist siege of 1529-1530, and when Cosimo I decided that he would strengthen them still further he distributed the work among a number of artists, including Benvenuto Cellini (who was also consulted on the fortification of Paris by the French King Francis I).

The mathematical interests of Italian art theorists were particularly suited to the development of a type of fortification based—to allow for a deftly exact flanking fire from the bastions—on geometrical principles. The cult of harmony, proportion

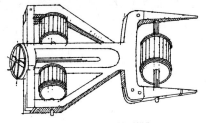

2 MARINE MISSILE

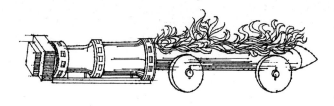

3 CANNON AND MISSILE COMBINED

and symmetry among 15th Century Italian artists and architects fitted this need for precisely angled fire and regular, coherent planning. Inasmuch as the interest of the architects was shared by humanist-minded princes, it is not surprising that in Italy more than anywhere else the reaction of plain military men to the need for a new type of fortification was systematized into a model that would be adapted elsewhere. Italian-style forts were erected not only in Europe and not only during the Renaissance; the star-shaped forts built to guard the mouth of the Mississippi in the War of 1812 would have appeared perfectly familiar to a Florentine engineer-architect of 1550.

In sum, the Italians were not lagging in military technology. They became the prey of foreigners for other reasons. They were unused to fighting in large armies made up of men from different states. Their leadership was divided as Italy was politically divided. Their generals were often hampered by civilian government agents who followed the armies to see that the generals did not waste money or take unnecessary risks. Finally, there was no widely felt urge to keep the foreigners out; the enemy of today might be the ally of tomorrow. With no pan-Italian policy, with no united military plan, it is not surprising that the determined monolithic powers forced the states of Italy to provide the ring and act as their seconds while they punched away for the dynastic championship of Europe.

The wars of the early 16th Century had no keener observer of both their political and military aspects than Machiavelli. He was 24 in 1494 and he died a month after the sack of Rome in 1527. From 1498 until his dismissal from office on the return of the Medici to Florence in 1512, he was a civil servant—not a very important one, but one whose office kept him near the center of important decisions. His principal duty was writing up and sending out instructions from the Ten of War, Florence's for-

eign relations committee. But he was no mere clerk; his own name appeared at the bottom of these instructions to foreign ambassadors. He also went on missions himself—but never the most sensitive ones. During his diplomatic career he had occasion to meet and speak with most of the important men of his time: the Kings of France and Germany, the Pope, military leaders from several countries and, of course, any number of Italian princes. At home Machiavelli was responsible for keeping in touch with Florentine armies in the field and for raising—this was a project of his own—a national militia of foot and horse in the Tuscan countryside.

An intensely energetic man of affairs, Machiavelli took to his pen only when leisure was forced on him. Because he shared his contemporaries' interest in Roman history he read much classical literature in the years of his unwilling retirement, and each book he produced carried a heavier freight of humanist reading and reflection. His works—on Livy's *History of Rome*, on the art of war, on Florentine history— came, in fact, to smell increasingly of the lamp, though the passion and originality of the man and his concern with current affairs contrived to give them a notable vitality. This, coupled with the taut, epigrammatic style that makes Machiavelli the finest of all Italian prose writers, has kept them alive today.

The Prince was his first book. It incorporates, in the formal guise of a treatise, his most urgent reflections on his personal experiences, his own observations of the Italian scene. It was written in 1513, a year after his dismissal from office, and was in fact not only the vehicle for his ideas on how Italy could recover her freedom but a way of showing the Medici—who had not yet disillusioned him by dismantling the republican constitution of Florence—that he was a man who deserved re-employment. If they had responded, they would have gained a valuable public servant and the world would probably have lost the later books which are an essential complement to *The Prince*. Machiavelli's main sympathies were republican, but this could not be guessed without reading the *Discourses* on Livy. *The Prince*, with its emphasis on expediency, is about how to deal with an emergency, not how to constitute an ideal city.

The main themes of *The Prince* are these: a state must have a national citizen army and not rely on mercenaries. It must have a resolute policy, backed to the hilt by cash and troops, unimpeded by delays in decision-making and flirtations with neutralist positions. Its rulers must resort to craft if the safety of the state demands it. A ruler cannot afford the luxury of a private conscience. An individual can afford to tell the truth and suffer for it; he suffers alone. But a ruler may not strike a noble gesture if the people he is responsible for are to suffer as a result.

All these themes were prompted by Machiavelli's own knowledge of affairs. The irresolution and treachery of the mercenary troops employed by Florence convinced him that national troops were the only answer—a solution buttressed by his interpretation of Roman history. On a mission to France in 1500, repeatedly snubbed or ignored as the representative of a weak state, he saw that a country was respected only when it was strong. Constantly hampered by the hesitant policy of his employers, he came to see that half measures (favored by the cautious businessmen of Florence) were useless, neutrality a form of suicide. From the French gibe that Florence was *Ser Nihilo*, "Mr. Nothing," he saw that in the modern world money and arms alone counted, and that in a life-and-death struggle a small man must sometimes hit a big bully below the belt. And these lessons were reinforced in 1502 by his meeting with Cesare Borgia, whose ruthlessness and deceit paid heavy dividends in his campaigns against the city-states of the Romagna. Subsequent missions to France demonstrated to him how a strong monarchy had made a fighting power out of the fickle and light-minded French, and this strengthened his opinion that Florence should be well armed and have a resolute ruler in whose policy there could be no place for scruple.

These lessons he spelled out in *The Prince*, supporting modern examples of political behavior with references to similar examples in ancient Greece and Rome. Men had written about statecraft all throughout the Middle Ages, but always in terms of what the Christian ruler *should* do. Machiavelli wrote of what rulers *had* to do to survive. Though statesmen had always flouted Christian morality when it suited them, the principle had never been openly stated before, let alone recommended. In *The Prince* we have for the first time a work that deals with politics as a study of the practical and expedient rather than of the ideal, and with history as a guide to conduct in the present.

One lesson of the wars was to show that the qualities that make for intellectual sophistication are not necessarily those that win wars. The subtle and civilized Italians were defeated by the culturally old-fashioned Spanish and French. The pragmatic merchant could not deal with the less rational *élan* of "feudal" warriors.

Though they were defeated, the Italians were not destroyed. Once the riots were over, the shops reopened and life went on. From a European point of view, perhaps the most lasting effect of the wars was that by observing them Machiavelli was led to codify the politics of expediency, and thereby to transform political theory into the companion rather than the conscience of political action. From Giotto to Leonardo, artists had sought to show how men really stood and moved; in one swift treatise Machiavelli showed how man, political man, really thought.

A FANFARE OF TRUMPETS *adds a characteristic Renaissance flourish to "The Baptism of the King," by the Venetian artist Carpaccio.*

THE CARNIVAL SPIRIT

The Renaissance was an age of spectacles, filled with the clash of festival sports, the pomp of processions, the tumult of great citywide celebrations. Almost any occasion—a saint's day, the arrival of a visiting prince, the anniversary of a great battle, even the dismissal of an ambassador—was reason to fill the streets with revelry. When there were no events, however trivial, to celebrate, the gaiety of the age found expression in hunts and ball games, horse races, boxing matches, snowball fights. Trumpeters like those above were the flamboyant heralds of the time, announcing town criers, accompanying brides to church, enlivening banquets or preceding nobles and dignitaries through the streets. In brief, the men of the Renaissance needed no excuse for celebration: they were busy celebrating life itself.

A CITY
IN PROCESSION

A Renaissance procession was a civic spectacle. It brought together in one majestic display a city's magnificently robed nobles, magistrates and leading citizens, its military companies, contingents of clergymen, and swarms of musicians, acrobats and jesters. Thousands marched while, from their doorways, windows or housetops, thousands more beheld the spectacle. Processions marked a variety of occasions. In the city-state of Siena, whose patron was the Virgin Mary, the Day of Assumption was celebrated by a spirited festival, portrayed in the 16th Century painting shown here. In the picture, colorfully costumed companies representing different wards of the city march around the Piazza del Campo. Each proudly follows a wheeled float built in the shape of its emblematic animal—a goose, snail, elephant or unicorn—amid the flurry of unfurling banners and the blare of trumpets.

Describing an occasion of similar splendor, the Feast of St. John in Florence, one spectator captured the festive spirit of the age: "The whole city," he wrote, "is given over to revelry and feasting . . . so that this whole earth seems like a paradise."

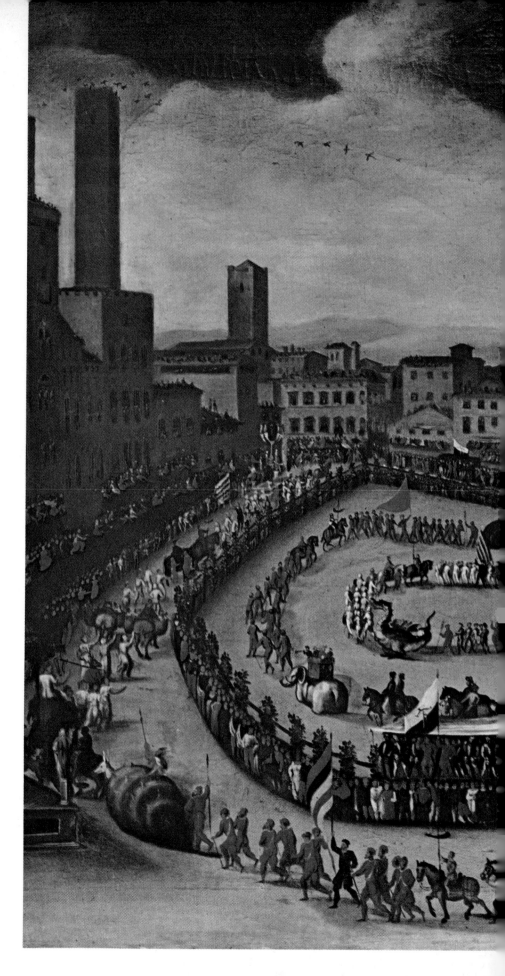

PLAYING BALL, *an Italian noblewoman prepares to swing her paddle. The game she is playing, "giuoco della palla," was a primitive form of tennis.*

GAMES FOR PLEASURE AND EXERCISE

The energy and enthusiasm of the Renaissance found expression in a wide variety of sports and games. Schoolmasters considered physical exercise an essential part of education and included it as a daily part of the curriculum. The Florentine prince Piero de' Medici played a popular ball game, like the one shown opposite, so passionately that he often let pressing affairs of state wait while he finished a match. According to the writer Leon Battista Alberti, exercise was both necessary for the young and useful for the old. The only people who do not exercise, he declared, are those "who do not wish to live happy, gladsome and sane."

A GAME OF CHESS, *a pastime popular in both court and tavern, was considered "a pleasing and ingenious amusement" when not played too seriously.*

A SNOWBALL FIGHT *offers outdoor sport for both lords and ladies in midwinter. The scene is from a 15th Century Italian fresco of the four seasons.*

THE SPLENDOR OF SPECTATOR SPORTS

Public sports, like the rough-and-tumble horse race, or Palio *(above)*, with which Florence honored its patron saint, were played in the streets and squares of all Renaissance cities. Each city had its traditional sports, and no festival was complete without the excitement of the games. Some places were famed for their bullfights, others for their jousts or donkey races. The regattas of Venice were known throughout Italy. In Pisa, the most popular sport was a mock battle on a bridge, commemorating a

historic defeat of the Saracens there. The Florentines were enthusiasts not only of the horse race but of boxing *(right)* and *palla al calcio*—a football game with 27 players on each team.

The pell-mell Palio was as popular in Siena as in Florence (it is still run in Siena today). The race was held even in periods when the city was threatened by invading armies—and in 1474, a year of war, gunpowder was actually taken from military supplies to provide fireworks for the Palio.

A HORSE RACE *through the streets of Florence, part of the city's annual celebration of the Feast of St. John, was a thrilling and hazardous event. Riders were often thrown and trampled and spectators injured as mounts thundered through the narrow streets.*

GENTEEL BOXERS, *three young Florentines engage in a local form of the sport called "civettino." In this game, combatants pinned down their opponents by treading on their feet. Then, at legs' length, they flailed away with their hands, ducking and dodging blows.*

MASKED MUSICIANS *sing to the accompaniment of a lute. In the Renaissance, musicians were often employed as part of a noble's domestic staff to play or sing at banquets and balls or between scenes of courtly shows.*

ACROBATS AND WRESTLERS *perform for a cluster of partying lords and ladies while lute players strum in the background. Such gatherings had a diversity of amusements, from impromptu acts to elaborate tableaux.*

ENTERTAINMENTS FOR THE ARISTOCRACY

Renaissance society was steeped in pageant. When musicians played *(opposite)*, they often wore masks and elaborate costumes. The antics of acrobats *(below)* enlivened the most formal courtly gatherings. At dinner parties, as one noble lady wrote, "the different dishes . . . were carried in to the sound of trumpets." When a troupe of actors performed, the play often mattered less to the audience than the costumes and scenery. Fantastic spectacles were staged between the acts. When the Cardinal of Ferrara presented a play in 1508—"a farce or merry jape," as one spectator described it—the most enthralling part was an interlude in which several winebibbing cooks danced about the stage beating on earthen pots. During these interludes, the stage might be filled with fireworks, torches, lifelike animal costumes or colorful birds. For special effect, performers might even set fire to the scenery.

THE NOBLE HUNT

The spectacles of city and court were matched by the pageantry of a Renaissance country hunt. The chase was "a true pastime for great lords," according to a popular handbook of manners. Indeed, a well-trained hunting falcon was considered

the finest gift anyone could give. Stores of wine and supplies of food were usually brought along as a company set out after deer or boar. For a lord, the only fit quarry was the full-grown stag; when a herd was spotted only the stag was hunted down. In Paolo Uccello's painting, above, patricians canter pleasantly on horseback and a retinue of huntsmen, kennelmen and beaters do the hard work on foot, in a scene that vividly expresses the pageantry and vitality of the age.

8

RENAISSANCE IN THE NORTH

The habits of thought and the cultural achievements associated with the Italian Renaissance achieved their full intensity in the first half of the 15th Century, the age of the great creative artists Masaccio and Donatello, Brunelleschi and Alberti. By this time the social conditions of Italy had enabled scholars and artists to produce a culture of supreme quality, and though Florence was the leader, this culture was common to the whole peninsula. What was reborn in the Renaissance was contact with the ideas of the ancient world. What made the period of this rebirth memorable was the existence of so many men of genius and a sustained burst of creative activity.

There was a fairly clear pattern to the development of the Italian Renaissance. Basic to the design was a new social and political order, whose educational and ethical needs were different from those of the medieval world. The emergence of humanism came as an answer to those needs. This led to the growth of a social and intellectual atmosphere in which genius could flourish—genius expressed in a triumphant rephrasing of man's deepest reactions to God, to love and to nature.

This pattern emerged much later in the rest of Europe. The central years of the Renaissance in Germany, France, England and Spain stretched over the 16th, even into the 17th Century.

These later outbursts of creative vigor followed the example of Italy, but even if Italy had not existed, or had been culturally numb, the other countries of Europe would have experienced cultural Renaissances of their own.

Each European country had had a vigorous national culture during the Middle Ages—as is evidenced by the German cathedrals, and by such poets as Geoffrey Chaucer in England and François Villon in France. Therefore, to speak of Renaissances in the north and in Spain is not to imply that these areas had been asleep and then suddenly woke up. It is to suggest that the 16th and early 17th Centuries saw the development of a culture markedly different in tone from that of the Middle Ages and expressed by an unprecedented emergence of men of genius.

The difference of tone was due in part to the example of Italy. But no country can learn from the

A RENAISSANCE LEGACY *can be traced in Rome's graceful Turtle Fountain. Created in 1585 in the vibrant Mannerist style, it recapitulated Renaissance art and pointed the way to the ornate splendor of the baroque.*

ideas of another until it is ready to do so. Other European nations snapped up Italy's humanism and its artistic styles as greedily as they did because the moment was right: the armies of these nations began to pour into Italy at the very time that the countries themselves were rapidly reaching a state of development that made possible a cultural leap forward.

It was not until the late 15th Century that the administrative and financial machines of the Western powers reached this point. Now, for the first time, they could send large armies outside their own borders. Well organized internally, domestic peace assured by strong monarchs, they could also provide a settled, reasonably prosperous environment in which secular education could absorb new ideas, and individuals explore new tastes. Travel, whether for business, diplomacy or scholarly reasons, had brought foreigners to Italy from the beginnings of the Renaissance, in the time of Giotto and Petrarch. Now, in the late 15th and early 16th Centuries, the soil in which these contacts had been planted was ready to produce a harvest.

Humanism itself does not equal Renaissance. Bringing to light the intellectual life of Greece and Rome did, it is true, enormously extend the range of ideas men could think about and the ways in which they could express their thoughts. But a Renaissance depended on the talent that could put these thoughts into enduring memorable form. In each country a body of humanist scholars prepared the way for more original, creative writers to express themselves in the new styles.

Not surprisingly, it was in Germany that Italian humanism made its first strong impact abroad. Though the empire as a whole was divided and incompetently administered, there were thriving towns with a degree of municipal independence that gave them a strong resemblance to the city-states of Italy. With their own schools and universities

THE GODDESS FORTUNE, *carrying reins and a chalice that symbolize her power to chastise and to reward man, makes her airborne rounds in this engraving by the German master Albrecht Dürer. The print's Renaissance characteristics—its mythological subject, its realistic nude figure, its use of perspective —were products of Dürer's studies in Italy. Here the artist, raised in the medieval tradition, heartily embraced Renaissance principles. Through his later essays, woodcuts and engravings, he did more than any other man to popularize the classical revival in his own homeland. Thus Dürer's visit to Italy in 1494 may be said to mark the start of the northern Renaissance.*

and with a merchant aristocracy that felt a need for advanced secular education, towns like Basel and Nürnberg learned readily from Italy. And, at the opposite pole, the emperor himself needed the eloquence of humanists for his diplomacy. He also enjoyed their ability to eulogize a ruler, an art they had learned in the service of Italian tyrant princes.

Thus, although the greatest humanist scholar and popularizer that northern Europe produced was a Dutch priest named Desiderius Erasmus, when Erasmus began to spread the gospel of humanism it was in Germany that he found the greatest number of congenial minds. Erasmus lived from 1466 to 1536. He traveled widely, made friends everywhere, and developed an enormous international correspondence through which he helped disseminate humanism throughout Europe. He also was able to take advantage of the newly invented art of printing and became, in fact, the first author to live on the profits of his books, and the first author to produce one bestseller after another. The invention of printing was, of course, another reason why Italian ideas spread so rapidly beyond the Alps after the late 15th Century.

The German Renaissance, while it was the first of the northern European Renaissances, was the shortest in duration. It flourished at the court of Maximilian I in the last years of the 15th and the first years of the 16th Century, after which it was sucked into the bitter theological controversies of the Reformation. Humanism, with its emphasis on the dignity of man's own works, was essentially a Catholic philosophy. The rise of Protestantism, with its special emphasis on man's intrinsically evil nature, brought the humanist movement in Germany to an end. But while it lasted it produced some great names: Johann Reuchlin, a Christian who was a scholar of the Hebrew language; Sebastian Brant, whose satirical verses in *The Ship of Fools* exercised a profound influence throughout

Europe in the late 15th Century; and Albrecht Dürer, the great painter and engraver.

Preparation for the French Renaissance began around 1500 with the work of the humanist scholars Jacques Lefèvre d'Etaples, who brought back the principles of humanism to France after a visit to Florence, and Guillaume Budé, who fostered the study of Greek works and was the moving spirit behind the establishment of the Collège de France by Francis I.

In terms of wide cultural achievement the French Renaissance spans the middle two generations of the 16th Century. In art it is associated with the work of Italian painters who were drawn to the court of Francis I, the first French monarch prepared to pay lavishly to satisfy his cultural interests. The result was the elegant, mannered and, above all, decorative art of the School of Fontainebleau. The group of poets headed by Joachim du Bellay and Pierre de Ronsard and known as La Pléiade was also active in France in the middle of the 16th Century, encouraging the use of French in literature and striving earnestly to enrich the language. François Rabelais' ribald and intellectually stimulating masterpiece *Gargantua* was published in 1534 and was an immediate and influential success. The *Essays* of Montaigne appeared almost half a century later.

In England and Spain there was an even greater gap between humanist preparation and literary and artistic achievement. Erasmus had humanist friends in England—Thomas More, author of *Utopia*, and John Colet, dean of St. Paul's and founder of St. Paul's School, among them. But the key figures in the English Renaissance were Edmund Spenser, Christopher Marlowe and William Shakespeare; behind their careers loomed England's first Renaissance court, that of Elizabeth I, who died in 1603. In Spain the University of Alcalá was founded in 1508 with a deliberately humanist program. But it was even longer before Spain achieved its constellation of great creative talents—the great painter El Greco (c.1541-1614), the novelist Miguel de Cervantes (1547-1616), the dramatist Lope de Vega (1562-1635).

To all these countries, as they slowly educated themselves into a new age, Italy acted as a challenging schoolmaster. Italian Neoplatonism influenced the way in which Colet thought about God, Spenser about love, Shakespeare about nature. Petrarch's sense of an intimate contact between himself and Cicero was echoed by Erasmus' sympathy for the ascetic scholar St. Jerome, author of the first Latin translation of the Bible. Petrarch's preoccupation with his own reactions to other people and to nature was copied by Elizabethan poets writing in a form dear to Petrarch himself, the sonnet. The humanists of the north listened intently to the message transmitted from Italy.

Humanist historical writing was one of Italy's most successful exports. Any self-made individual who feels that he has reached a pinnacle of fortune begins to think about providing himself with a pedigree (even if it is a faked one). It is the same with nations; there is a moment at which they wish to see their history written out in a fair hand, a record of difficulties overcome, of hazards faced and solved. This demands a new kind of historiography which keeps the intervention of God at a distance while showing how man has solved his own problems. Such a school of historiography was founded in France by Paolo Emilio of Verona who wrote an accurate history of his adopted country in 1516-1519. In England the founder was another Italian, Polydore Vergil, whose patronage by Henry VII enabled him to write a 26-volume history; in its secular regard for facts this work profoundly affected later English historical thinking—and ultimately the view of the English past presented by Shakespeare in his historical plays.

The Italians had much more to offer than historical models or the sonnet, or realism in painting, or classical proportions in architecture. Their attempts to provide accurate texts of ancient authors, their praise of the active, virtuous, secular life, and their attempt to show how much in the teaching of ancient philosophers was in anticipation of God's verbatim teaching through the mouth of Christ—all this was directly useful to northern humanists, who were mainly concerned with how to live good, useful lives in the world outside the church. Thomas More and Erasmus did not become Christian humanists simply because they read books written by Italians, but they were able to express themselves more clearly and forcibly because of the preparatory work that had been done in Italy. Though the tone of More's *Utopia*, and the topics it dealt with—war and peace, social justice —reflected More's own ideas about what needed reforming in his own society, the concept of the ideal community came from Plato, as did his emphasis on the control of man's political and social environment by reason. Plato, of course, had been rediscovered by the Italians. Erasmus' Biblical criticism was based on the Latin of the Vulgate, St. Jerome's Bible, which in turn was based on the method developed by Italian philologists in purifying the classic Roman texts.

Italy's schoolmaster phase may be divided into two periods. First the northern powers used Italians themselves as teachers. They imported artists —Andrea del Sarto was at the French court in 1518-1519 and Leonardo died there in the latter year. Pietro Torrigiano (who had broken Michelangelo's nose for him in a youthful brawl) completed the graceful tomb of Henry VII in Westminster Abbey in 1519. Italian diplomats and letter writers were used by the chanceries of England, France, Germany and Poland.

In the second period native pupils carried on in the Italian manner, and though Italians were called

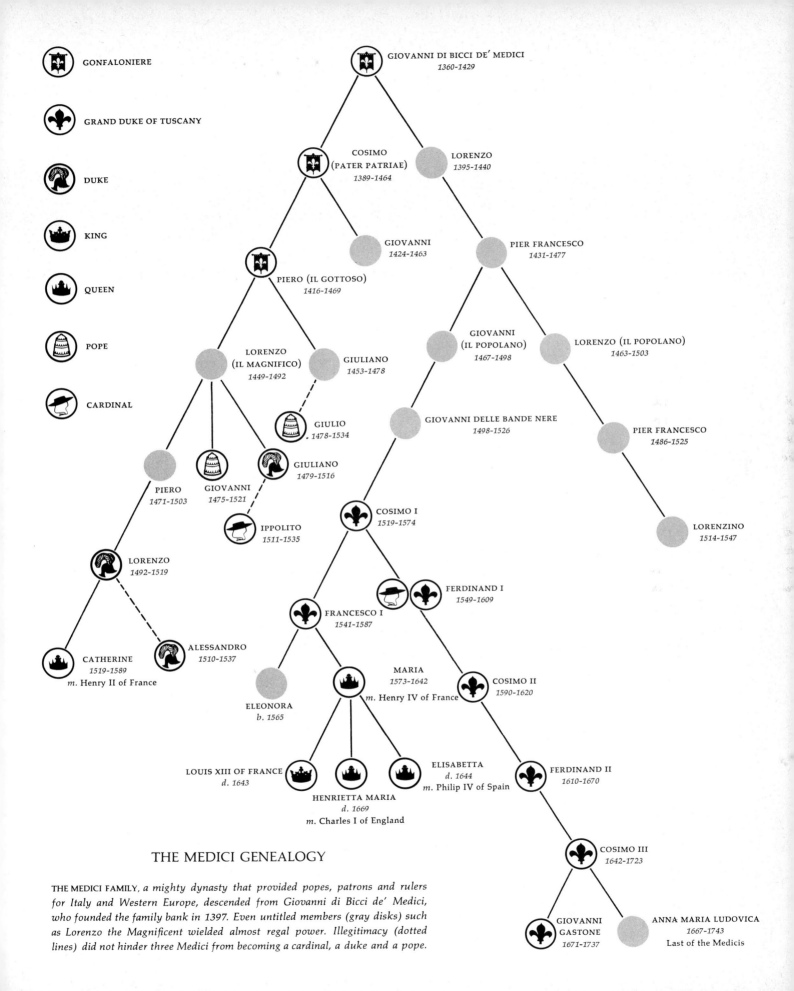

GONFALONIERE

GRAND DUKE OF TUSCANY

DUKE

KING

QUEEN

POPE

CARDINAL

GIOVANNI DI BICCI DE' MEDICI
1360-1429

COSIMO
(PATER PATRIAE)
1389-1464

LORENZO
1395-1440

GIOVANNI
1424-1463

PIER FRANCESCO
1431-1477

PIERO (IL GOTTOSO)
1416-1469

GIOVANNI
(IL POPOLANO)
1467-1498

LORENZO (IL POPOLANO)
1463-1503

LORENZO
(IL MAGNIFICO)
1449-1492

GIULIANO
1453-1478

GIOVANNI DELLE BANDE NERE
1498-1526

PIER FRANCESCO
1486-1525

GIULIO
1478-1534

PIERO
1471-1503

GIOVANNI
1475-1521

GIULIANO
1479-1516

IPPOLITO
1511-1535

COSIMO I
1519-1574

LORENZINO
1514-1547

LORENZO
1492-1519

FERDINAND I
1549-1609

CATHERINE
1519-1589
m. Henry II of France

ALESSANDRO
1510-1537

FRANCESCO I
1541-1587

MARIA
1573-1642
m. Henry IV of France

COSIMO II
1590-1620

ELEONORA
b. 1565

LOUIS XIII OF FRANCE
d. 1643

ELISABETTA
d. 1644
m. Philip IV of Spain

FERDINAND II
1610-1670

HENRIETTA MARIA
d. 1669
m. Charles I of England

COSIMO III
1642-1723

THE MEDICI GENEALOGY

THE MEDICI FAMILY, *a mighty dynasty that provided popes, patrons and rulers for Italy and Western Europe, descended from Giovanni di Bicci de' Medici, who founded the family bank in 1397. Even untitled members (gray disks) such as Lorenzo the Magnificent wielded almost regal power. Illegitimacy (dotted lines) did not hinder three Medici from becoming a cardinal, a duke and a pope.*

GIOVANNI
GASTONE
1671-1737

ANNA MARIA LUDOVICA
1667-1743
Last of the Medicis

in from time to time, it was as gifted individuals rather than as the only accredited representatives of an essential part of the curriculum of modern life. It was not long before the pupils were challenging their former teachers. Catherine de' Medici, Dowager Queen of France after the death of her husband, Henry II, summoned Italian artists to her court to help create an atmosphere similar to that in which she had grown up. But French master masons and artisans would no longer unquestioningly accept Italian designs, and the result, visible in tapestries, enamels, jewelry, architecture and books of the 16th Century, is a happy wedding of French and Italian influences.

In the arts, the greatest Italian influences were literary ones. Climate as well as national tradition led to a fairly cautious acceptance of Italian architecture, and the most direct influence did not come from such innovators as Brunelleschi and Michelangelo but, late in the 16th Century, from Andrea Palladio, with his emphasis on classic symmetry. In painting, northern Europe, though conservative, had such vitality that it had already given something to Italy itself—notably the technique of painting in oils. Knowledge of this technique filtered up from Naples, where Flemish painters were working before the mid-15th Century, and influenced artists in northern Italy by the 1480s. Although Dürer did study for a while in Italy and acted as an interpreter of Italian ideas for Germany, the artistic conventions of the north tended to hold their own: Holbein's *Henry VIII* stood in a sufficiently stout three-dimensionality for early Tudor taste, which ran to the sturdy and the comfortable rather than the fragile and the flamboyant.

But the Italian influence on books was really pervasive. Italian literature covered an extraordinarily wide range of form and mood. Not only did it resurrect classical forms like the dialogue, the tragedy and the epic, but it developed the medieval short story with such gusto that northern novelists and dramatists raided Boccaccio and Matteo Bandello for plots well into the 17th Century. Not only did Italy have a respectful attitude to Vergil and Ovid but it also took seriously a body of vernacular works—by such writers as Dante, Boccaccio and Petrarch—which, after a period of neglect, came by the 15th Century to constitute a parallel body of Italian-language "classics."

As a result, many major Italian writers turned to the classical tradition for form but to the vernacular tradition for tone. This combination of secure form and vital content gave Italian works a special appeal to lively creative minds throughout Europe. Moreover, alongside the confident, racy tone of much Italian literature was a note of nostalgic melancholy. Renaissance Italy had its melancholics as well as its enthusiasts; the buoyant civic politician, whose hero was Cicero, was balanced by the recluse, whose love of the slower tempi of the countryside was supported by Vergil in the mood of his *Bucolics* and by the Arcadian musings of Theocritus.

The early idyllic novels such as *Arcadia* by England's Sir Philip Sidney, and the Spaniard Jorge de Montemayor's *Diana*, all of which put well-born lords and ladies into a tranquil rural setting of woods and meadows, sheep and gentle shepherds, could not have been written without the Italian example of Jacopo Sannazzaro's *Arcadia* (1504). And Sannazzaro in turn depended on Theocritus —but on Theocritus with a difference. Whereas the characters in Theocritus' writings were simple peasants and other rough-hewn types, Sannazzaro introduced world-weary courtiers into a rustic scene, and in this way so modified his model that it appealed to a feeling more characteristic of the urbane Renaissance than of the simpler classical world.

Similarly the Italian dramatists, while using the act-divisions and other devices employed by the

Roman playwrights Plautus, Terence and Seneca, elaborated the love interest and made the comic relief mirror contemporary society; once again, a classical product was modernized in Italy and made suitable for export. Italian literary influence was strong because it brought attractively up to date so much of what men had thought about not only in antiquity but in the Middle Ages. The Italian influence was therefore complicated, but it was strong precisely because it *was* complicated. If it had consisted merely of ancient literature in translation, the national literary traditions in other countries would have resisted its influence and gone their own way.

Moreover, Italian influence was at hand not only when writers in other countries were considering into what mold—novel, epic, play, lyric—they were to pour their feelings, but also when they were trying to decide what language they would use. There were several choices of language open to Italian authors. If they chose to write in Latin they could limit themselves to words used by Cicero— the most generally admired stylist—or they could fall back on the usage of a variety of other classical authors. If they chose to write in Italian they could use pure 14th Century Tuscan, or an Italian which picked and chose words from many different regions and even from Latin itself.

As time passed, this wealth of choices began more and more to be a question of which vernacular to use. That the problem came up at the time it did is important, for it started arguments about language elsewhere in Europe just when modern French, Spanish and English were in the process of crystallizing themselves.

Ultimately the Italian emphasis on the vernacular prevented other languages from being swamped with Latin words and phrases. Castiglione, for example, talked about language in *The Courtier*. When this work was translated into English in

MEANWHILE IN THE NORTH . . .

In the 16th Century, when Florence had long been established as a second Athens in the eyes of the Western world, Ivan IV *(above)*, a domineering young duke, came to the throne of a Russia still mired in feudal despotism. He was the grandson of Grand Duke Ivan III of Moscow, who had laid the foundations for a new nation by his refusal in 1480 to pay tribute to the Tatars, Russia's longtime overlords. In the following years, as the Tatars warred among themselves, Ivan III established Moscow's domination over a vast territory. Ultimately, he proclaimed himself "Sovereign of all Russia." To glorify his capital, he imported architects and painters from Renaissance Italy. Finally, in 1547, Ivan IV, known as "The Terrible," formally adopted the august title of Czar, or Caesar.

A tall, fierce man subject to ungovernable fits of rage, Ivan IV suppressed the old landed aristocracy, the boyars. In his later years, as Russian armies conquered Kazan and Astrakhan in Asia, and advanced into Siberia, distrust and terror became Ivan's policy. He had the saintly metropolitan of Moscow, the head of the Russian Church, strangled for opposing him. He killed his own son, whom he loved, in a rage. Three years later, in 1584, Ivan the Terrible died in a fit of delirium.

1561, it contained a letter from Sir John Cheke, an ardent, if cranky, disciple of a pure national language. "I am of this opinion," Cheke wrote, "that our tongue should be written clean and pure, unmixed and unmangled with borrowing of other tongues." Almost certainly Shakespeare's English would have been less directly and idiomatically English had it not been for the influence of Dante's and Boccaccio's Italian on the language theorists of the 15th and early 16th Centuries, and the respectability they gave to a comparatively unlatinized vernacular.

The direct influence of Renaissance political thought outside Italy is difficult to trace. It consisted, above all, of the influence of Machiavelli, whose name by the second half of the 16th Century had become an epithet: a "Machiavel" was anyone you hated, particularly if you wanted to suggest that he was crafty and irreligious. But, alongside the name-calling, there was serious study of his works. *The Prince* was circulated in manuscript in England long before 1640 when it was first allowed to be printed there, and more than one ruler used it to justify what he was planning to do anyway.

However, despite the widespread attention paid to Machiavelli's writings in the 16th Century it is impossible to point to any one political action that depended on a knowledge of his works. Politicians react to events, not to books—or at least this was true until Marx published *Das Kapital*. But a book can help formulate the creed of a party, and action can flow from that. Something like this happened during the Puritan Oliver Cromwell's ascendancy in England between 1640 and 1660, but England was in the throes of experimenting with republican forms of government at the time. With hereditary kingship temporarily abolished, the nation needed the guidance of republican experts in practicable, rather than legally correct political expedi-

ents. The necessary information was obtained from Dutch and French Huguenot theorists, as well as from Machiavelli. The states of Europe took from Machiavelli what they needed, when they needed it, but their political and religious circumstances were so different from those of Machiavelli's Italy that they needed very little.

What Europe did need, and took a lot of, was the teachings of Castiglione. The nobility wanted a program that would bring the values of chivalry up to date: the expanding bourgeoisie wanted a way of life that would carry with it some upward mobility in the social and cultural sphere. *The Courtier* was a bestseller throughout Europe. In fact, after religious works, one of the largest categories of 16th Century books was that dealing with social behavior. The historian Ruth Kelso has counted 891 volumes. dealing solely with the education and conduct of women—and most of these derived from (and some did little more than paraphrase) *The Courtier* and Giovanni della Casa's *Galateo*. Slipping beneath the guard of politics and religion, the Italian program of individual self-culture was able to affect the tone of social life even under the nose of a divine-right monarch or a Protestant church.

Italian influence on the rest of Europe would not have been so great if the creativity of the Renaissance had suddenly petered out early in the 16th Century. Just as a teacher who has the vitality to continue with his own original work is more respected than one who lives on the reputation of what he has achieved in the past, Italy the schoolmaster continued to impress Europe with its creative powers.

In one branch of cultural activity, indeed, Italy displayed more creative vigor in the 16th Century than in any earlier period. This was music. Italy and the Netherlands were the countries where "the new music" came to the full pitch of its develop-

LUTE

"SPINETTINO"

PSALTERY

"LIRA DA BRACCIO"

MUSICAL INSTRUMENTS *were indispensable accessories to Renaissance life. Every cultured person was expected to play at least one. The psaltery, "spinettino" and "lira da braccio" were played in gardens, ballrooms and churches. But the most popular instrument, the lute, was heard everywhere, delighting Tuscan peasants and Sienese lords alike. Great lute players were so esteemed that Isabella d'Este protected her favorite from punishment after he murdered his wife.*

ment in the careers of Giovanni da Palestrina and Orlando di Lasso, both of whom wrote motets, Masses and other choral music.

Music and song had always played a part in Italian life, both in church and outside. But from the second half of the 15th Century an interest in its potentiality quickened. Marsilio Ficino learned to play the lyre; Leonardo impressed Lodovico Sforza with his musical talents as much as with his artistic ones. From pictures like Titian's *The Concert* and Raphael's *St. Cecilia* we can see something of the charm and the philosophic dignity that music had for contemporaries. With its many courts and its sophisticated attitudes toward cultivated leisure, it was natural that secular music should flourish more happily in Italy than elsewhere.

In Italy, too, the prestige of poetry and a generally sensuous approach to the arts helped bring about the major revolutions in Renaissance music. These were the expressive wedding of music to verse, and the substitution of one kind 'of musical texture for another: instead of separate strands of music laid one on top of the other, there was now harmony—i.e., vertical chords, rather than a set of horizontal lines.

To gain richness and diversity of expression, choirs were made large, new instruments were introduced, composers experimented with dissonances and quarter tones. Nicola Vicentino of Ferrara even constructed a harpsichord which had not 12 but 31 tones for each octave. Both in the papal chapel and in the musical academies which were created for the performance and discussion of music in the Italian cities, the emphasis was on how to bring back to music the expressiveness, the power to move, that it had had among the Greeks. No Greek music remained. But no Greek painting remained either—as far as was known then—and yet Italians had gone to literary sources and then set about mastering the realistic techniques which would enable them to reproduce what they decided Greek painting must have looked like. It was the same with music. The Renaissance musicologist, E. E. Lowinsky, has noted: "Greek writings on music were studied by Renaissance musicians with the same awe and reverence as the philosophers studied Plato, the sculptors ancient statues, and the architects the remaining ancient buildings . . . The study of Greek ideas on music was used as a catalyst to bring about those radical changes in the aims and means of music that introduced a new epoch. The authority of ancient Greece was invoked to unseat the universal rule of counterpoint that had been reigning . . . for half a millennium."

The beginnings of opera, too, came from Italy; Claudio Monteverdi's *L'incoronazione di Poppea* (1642), which can still move a modern audience, was preceded by plays set to music, like the *Dafne* of Ottavio Rinuccini and Jacopo Peri (1594).

In the visual arts Europe saw no hint of Italian faltering. Titian painted with increasing power until his death in 1576, and Tintoretto produced a flow of astonishingly original work up to his death in 1594. By this time new names had appeared which were to become household words, and for two and a half centuries eclipse the fame of the masters of the *quattrocento*. In the eyes of connoisseurs of the 17th and 18th Centuries even Leonardo and Michelangelo lacked appeal when compared with Domenichino and Guido Reni, and the Carracci family, Lodovico, Agostino and Annibale, who, though fine artists and the best of their day, have never since, by popular taste, been considered comparable to the great masters. And just as Italy in the second generation of the 16th Century produced Mannerism, the first truly international style since the Gothic—for it appealed to aristocratic taste everywhere—so later in the century, with the work of Palladio and Vincenzo Scamozzi, Italy produced the first post-Gothic international style

in architecture, that of classicism. When to this we add the lively *novelle* of Bandello, which were published in the 1550s, and Torquato Tasso's immensely successful epic of 1581, *Gerusalemme Liberata*, we can see that to 16th Century Europe the Italian schoolmaster remained very much alive; his lessons continued to be taken with the seriousness due one who seemed at the height of his powers.

Much of this occurred beyond a time when rebirth had any meaning for Italy, but the significance of the Italian Renaissance and its power to infect the culture of other countries cannot be understood unless some attention is paid to its afterglow. Only by seeing how 16th and early-17th Century Europe turned for inspiration to the artists and scholars of this divided, defeated, but stubbornly creative country can we realize how great a debt our own culture owes to Italy.

Because that country gave unrivaled opportunities to talent over some two and a half centuries, a set of attitudes to life and to the arts was worked into a shape that enabled others, when they were ready, to absorb them as a tonic to their own aspirations. Each country, when it was prepared to step over the shadowy fissure that divided the medieval from the modern world, could reach out to grasp the steadying hand of Italy. While Italy did not affect the main course of political and economic events, it helped the whole modern world to think and feel and build and play.

If the Italian Renaissance had never happened, Shakespeare would probably still have written plays, Louis XIV would still have built a palace at Versailles, John Harvard would still have founded a college. But no Romeo and Juliet would have loved and died in Verona, there would have been no columns at Versailles, and Latin and Greek would not have helped to mold the imaginations of the Founding Fathers of America.

THE CHILD: *"To him it is granted to have whatever he chooses, to be whatever he wills"—Pico della Mirandola (1463-1494).*

A NEW VIEW OF MAN

As the great sculptor Donatello labored over a lifelike statue, he was heard exhorting it, "Speak then! Why will you not speak!" In a figurative sense, Donatello's statues, and many by other Renaissance masters, *do* speak: they state eloquently in stone and bronze the bold new attitude toward man that animated the age. The sculptured portraits reveal a new fascination and esteem for the individual. The full-bodied figures express an unabashed delight in the human form. Renaissance sculpture also asserts the vital optimism of the time. In Desiderio da Settignano's statue of a bright-eyed boy *(above)*, can be seen the same feeling that Count Pico della Mirandola put into words: "God the Father endowed man, from birth, with the seeds of every possibility and every life."

How fair is youth that flies so fast!

Then be happy, you who may;

what's to come is still unsure.

—LORENZO DE' MEDICI

Renaissance artists delighted in portraying youth. The Neapolitan sculptor Giovanni da Nola, seeking a figure to personify Temperance, chose to carve a lovely maiden *(right)*, alluring and sensuous, yet childlike in her purity. Similarly, a vision of perfect young manhood inspired Michelangelo as he planned his memorials to Giuliano and Lorenzo de' Medici, the son and grandson of Lorenzo the Magnificent. Transcending realistic portraiture, Michelangelo glorified Giuliano *(left)* as the ideal nobleman, and Lorenzo as the archetypical man of thought.

When these lordly figures were finished, the sculptor was told by a fatuous acquaintance that his statues were not good likenesses. Michelangelo, confident that his works would be immortal, replied: "Who will care, a thousand years hence, whether these are their features or not?"

Bring to me my kind, compassionate lady for company....

Let her chaste appearance, her modest words calm me.

—LORENZO DE' MEDICI

In the liberal spirit of the Renaissance, women of aristocratic families were accorded new respect and greater opportunities. As girls, some received the classical education given to their brothers. But all were brought up to be good mothers; the relief shown opposite, a Madonna and Child by the Florentine sculptor Desiderio da Settignano, reflects a growing sentimentality toward motherhood and children.

To fulfill her other roles, the well-born woman raised leisure to an art. The bust at right, another work by Desiderio, displays the grace and refinement expected of the lady as a dutiful wife, an occasional companion to her husband, a skillful hostess to his guests. A few gifted women, flowering in the hothouse of court society, became towering figures, and as versatile as the age's "universal man." One great lady, Vittoria Colonna, fascinated worldly courtiers, befriended religious rebels (for which she was placed under surveillance by a Church court), exchanged passionate lyrics with Michelangelo and secretly dispensed political advice to Pope Paul III.

Advance then, and…you may make yourself known to all the world.

—BOCCACCIO

Maturity came early to Renaissance man, bringing with it a driving ambition to win fame. Giovanni delle Bande Nere was one of many noblemen who fought as *condottieri* for glory and cash. This bold commander, portrayed above by Francesco da Sangallo, fell in a skirmish and died at the age of 28. Another mercenary, Duke Gianfrancesco Gonzaga II of Mantua, lived to enjoy his battle-won wealth and to sit for a bust *(far left)* by Gian Cristoforo Romano, which shows him in his virile middle years. But the rewards of commerce were safer and surer than the wages of war. The Florentine merchant Pietro Mellini, having amassed an impressive fortune, used it freely to assure his remembrance as a patron of the arts. His portrait *(left)*, by Benedetto da Maiano, reveals a wise old man who bears his wrinkles with a trace of wry humor.

It is a remarkable fact that we all must die,

and yet we all live as if we were to live forever.

—GUICCIARDINI

The Renaissance was a turbulent epoch in which death awaited young and old at every turn. Guidarello Guidarelli, the heroic warrior portrayed at right in a funerary statue by Tullio Lombardo, survived many a battle only to die in his prime at an assassin's hand. Yet always the age's passion for life made death seem remote. Pope Paul III, seen above in a bust by Guglielmo della Porta, led a long, full life as a worldly prince, lavish in his nepotism and his patronage of the arts; when he died at 81 he was vigorously pursuing a second life as a pontiff dedicated to Church reform. Even before his death, the Italian Renaissance may be said to have died. But its exuberant culture, carried abroad by teachers, writers and artists, took root in the north and shaped the quality of life in many nations. And its unconquerable vitality bequeathed to modern man "the seeds of every possibility and every life."

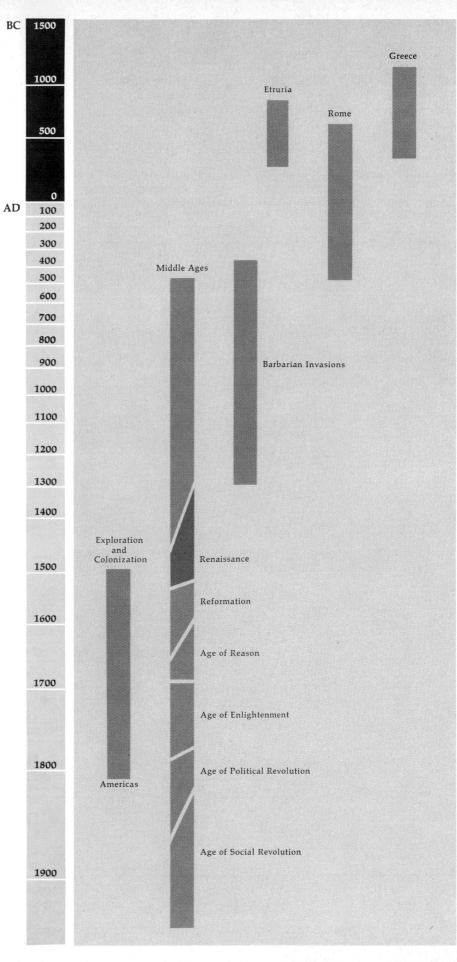

GREAT AGES
OF WESTERN
CIVILIZATION

The chart at right is designed to show the duration of the Renaissance in Italy, which forms the subject of this volume, and to relate it to the other cultures of the Western world that are considered in one major group of volumes of this series. This chart is excerpted from a comprehensive world chronology which appears in the introductory booklet to the series. Comparison of the chart seen here with the world chronology will enable the reader to relate the great ages of Western civilization to important cultures in other parts of the world.

On the following two pages is printed a chronological table of the important events that took place within the Italian peninsula during the era covered by this book.

CHRONOLOGY: *A listing of events significant in the history of the Italian Renaissance*

Thought and Culture

c. 1300	Humanism arises in Padua
1300	Giovanni Villani, Florentine banker, begins to write his *Chronicle*
c. 1306	Giotto completes the Arena Chapel frescoes, in Padua
1321	Dante dies, having completed *Divine Comedy*
1334	Giotto designs Florence's belltower
1336	Andrea Pisano designs first set of bronze doors for Florentine Baptistery
1341	Petrarch, first great humanist, crowned poet laureate at Rome
1353	Giovanni Boccaccio, founder of Italian prose, completes the *Decameron*
1392	Coluccio Salutati, chancellor of Florence, discovers Cicero's *Familiar Letters*
1397	Manuel Chrysoloras, Byzantine scholar, introduces Greek literature at University of Florence
1401	Ghiberti wins competition for design of second set of Baptistery doors
1401	Leonardo Bruni, Florentine writer, popularizes term *humanitas*
c. 1403	Brunelleschi and Donatello go to Rome to study ancient ruins
1415	Florentine humanist Poggio Bracciolini discovers classical manuscripts
c. 1415-17	Donatello carves statue of *St. George*
1419	Brunelleschi designs dome for Florence's cathedral
1423	Vittorino da Feltre establishes his school at Mantua
c. 1427	Masaccio paints *Tribute Money*
1429	Guarino establishes his school at Ferrara
1436	Leon Battista Alberti writes first treatise on theory of painting
1440	Lorenzo Valla writes exposé of the *Donation of Constantine*
c. 1440-42	Donatello casts *David*, first freestanding nude figure since antiquity
c. 1440-50	Fra Angelico paints the *Annunciation*
1447	Pope Nicholas V founds the Vatican library
c. 1452	Alberti writes *De re aedificatoria*, first modern work on architecture
1453	Mino da Fiesole carves earliest surviving Renaissance portrait bust
1453	Constantinople falls to Turks; many scholarly refugees come to Italy, bringing Greek manuscripts
c. 1455	Uccello paints the *Battle of San Romano*

1300 · 1350 · 1400 · 1450

PROTO-RENAISSANCE

GROWTH OF THE CITY-STATES

Politics and Society

1305	"Babylonian Captivity" begins; popes leave Rome to settle in Avignon
c. 1310	Venetian galleys begin maritime trade with Flanders and England
1313	Emperor Henry VII loses Lombardy; northern Italy independent
1338	Venice begins territorial expansion on mainland
1340s	Economic reversals and business depression beset Italy
1342	Walter of Brienne becomes Florentine despot, expelled the following year
1347	Cola di Rienzo rules briefly in Rome as Tribune of the People
1348	Black Death strikes Florence, seriously reduces the population
1350-55	Venice is defeated by Genoa; temporarily loses Black Sea supremacy
1354-67	Cardinal Albornoz partially restores pope's authority over Papal States
1378	Papacy returns to Rome from Avignon; Urban VI elected Pope
1378	Election of antipope Clement VII at Avignon starts Great Schism
1380	Venice defeats Genoa, becomes mistress of Levantine trade
1397	Medici bank is founded in Florence
1402	Gian Galeazzo Visconti, Duke of Milan, dies; his domain crumbles
1414-17	Council of Constance ends Great Schism
1417	Martin V becomes Pope; strengthens his sway over Papal States
1434	Cosimo de' Medici begins 30-year domination of Florence
1442	Naples and Sicily come under rule of Spanish House of Aragon
1450	Francesco Sforza, *condottiere* son-in-law of Duke Filippo Maria, conquers Milan, becomes Duke
1454	Peace of Lodi ushers in 40 years of relative peace among Italian states
1458	Pius II (Aeneas Silvius Piccolomini), humanist, becomes Pope

1475

1462 Platonic Academy, headed by Marsilio Ficino, is founded in Florence

1465 First Italian printing press is set up at Subiaco, near Rome

1479-99 Reign of Lodovico Sforza marks Golden Age of Renaissance in Milan
c. 1480 Botticelli paints the *Birth of Venus*
c. 1482 Leonardo da Vinci goes to work at the court of Lodovico Sforza
1486 Pico della Mirandola, humanist, writes *Oration on the Dignity of Man*
1490 Verrocchio's statue of *Condottiere Colleoni* is cast
1490 Aldine press at Venice is established by Aldus Manutius

c. 1495-98 Leonardo da Vinci paints the *Last Supper*

1500

c. 1503-05 Leonardo paints the *Mona Lisa*
1504 Michelangelo completes statue of *David*
1504 Sannazzaro's pastoral romance, *Arcadia*, is published
1506 Bramante draws his design for St. Peter's
1506 *Laocoön* sculpture is discovered
1508 Michelangelo begins to paint ceiling of Sistine Chapel
c. 1510-11 Raphael paints his masterpiece, the *School of Athens*, for the Vatican

1525

c. 1513 Raphael paints the *Sistine Madonna*
1513 Machiavelli writes *The Prince*
1515 Francis I of France begins bringing Italian artists to work at his court
1516 Ariosto's epic, *Orlando Furioso*, is published
c. 1518 Titian paints the *Bacchanal*
c. 1520 Mannerism style of painting emerges
1524-34 Michelangelo carves figures for tombs in Medici Chapel

1528 Castiglione's *The Courtier* is published
1536-40 Guicciardini writes *The History of Italy*
1536-41 Michelangelo paints the *Last Judgment*, in the Sistine Chapel
1543 Copernicus publishes his work on the solar system
1543 Vesalius publishes his work on human anatomy
1551 Giovanni da Palestrina is master of choirboys at St. Peter's
1554 Benvenuto Cellini completes bronze *Perseus*

1558 Giovanni della Casa's *Galateo* is published posthumously

1463 Venice begins 16-year war with the Turks
1469 Lorenzo de' Medici heads Florentine state
1471 Sixtus IV becomes Pope, turns the Papal States into a strong dominion
1478 Pazzi conspiracy against Medici fails
1479 Venice, defeated by Turkey, is forced to pay for trading privileges
1479 Lodovico Sforza seizes control of Milan from his nephew Gian Galeazzo
1484 Innocent VIII becomes Pope

1492 Alexander VI (Rodrigo Borgia) becomes Pope
1492 Lorenzo de' Medici dies
1494 Charles VIII of France invades Italy, marking beginning of foreign invasions

1494 Medici are driven from Florence; their bank is in virtual bankruptcy
1494-97 Savonarola is in power in Florence
1495 Charles VIII enters Naples as conqueror
1496 French are ousted from Naples by Spanish troops
1498 Savonarola is burned at the stake for heresy
1499 Louis XII of France launches second invasion of Italy, conquers Milan

1502 French and Spanish in Italy fall out, go to war
1503 Pope Alexander VI dies; his son Cesare Borgia loses political power
1503 Julius II, art patron, becomes Pope
1504 Spain conquers Kingdom of Naples, controls southern Italy

c. 1510 Venetian trade begins to decline as result of discovery of new route to Indies
1512 French defeat Spanish and papal forces at Ravenna
1512 Medici power is restored in Florence
1512 Swiss conquer Milan; install Maximilian Sforza as Duke
1513 Leo X, son of Lorenzo de' Medici, becomes Pope
1515 Francis I of France invades Italy
1515 French recover Milan after defeating Swiss at Battle of Marignano

1519 Charles I of Spain is elected Holy Roman Emperor Charles V

1525 French in Italy are defeated by Spanish at Battle of Pavia
1527 Rome is sacked by troops of the Holy Roman Empire
1527 Medici are expelled from Florence, republic temporarily restored
1535 Death of Francesco II (the last Sforza) brings Milan under Spanish rule

1555 Henry II of France invades Italy
1556 Philip II becomes King of Spain and ruler of Milan, Naples and Sicily
1559 By Treaty of Cateau-Cambrésis, France formally abandons its claims in Italy

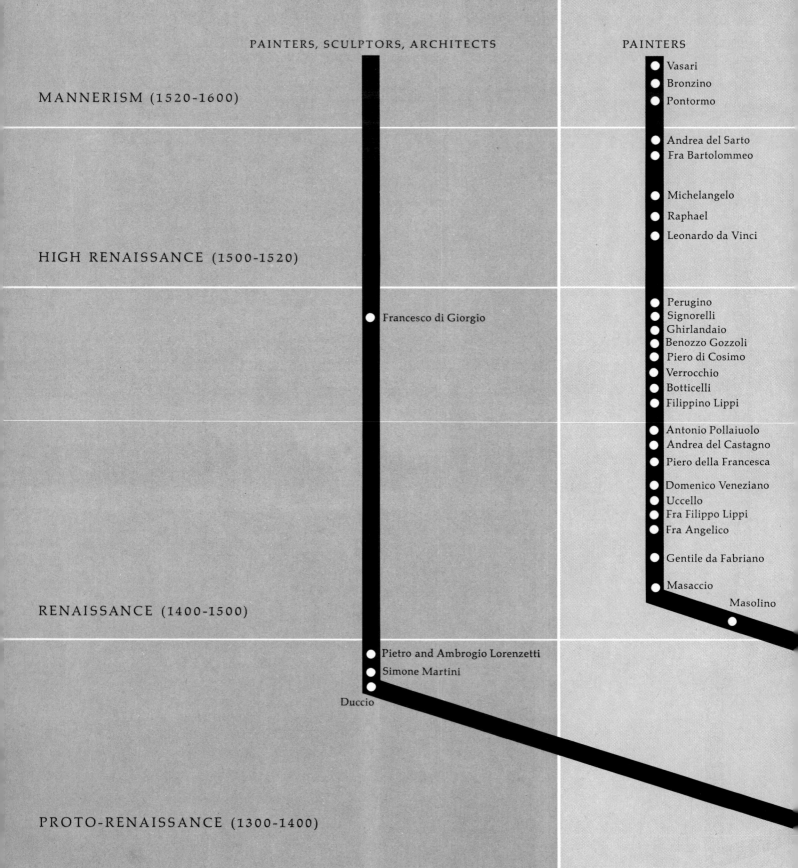

SIENA

PAINTERS, SCULPTORS, ARCHITECTS

PAINTERS

MANNERISM (1520-1600)

- Vasari
- Bronzino
- Pontormo

- Andrea del Sarto
- Fra Bartolommeo

- Michelangelo
- Raphael
- Leonardo da Vinci

HIGH RENAISSANCE (1500-1520)

- Francesco di Giorgio

- Perugino
- Signorelli
- Ghirlandaio
- Benozzo Gozzoli
- Piero di Cosimo
- Verrocchio
- Botticelli
- Filippino Lippi

- Antonio Pollaiuolo
- Andrea del Castagno
- Piero della Francesca

- Domenico Veneziano
- Uccello
- Fra Filippo Lippi
- Fra Angelico

- Gentile da Fabriano

- Masaccio

Masolino

RENAISSANCE (1400-1500)

- Pietro and Ambrogio Lorenzetti
- Simone Martini

Duccio

PROTO-RENAISSANCE (1300-1400)

FLORENCE

THE NORTH

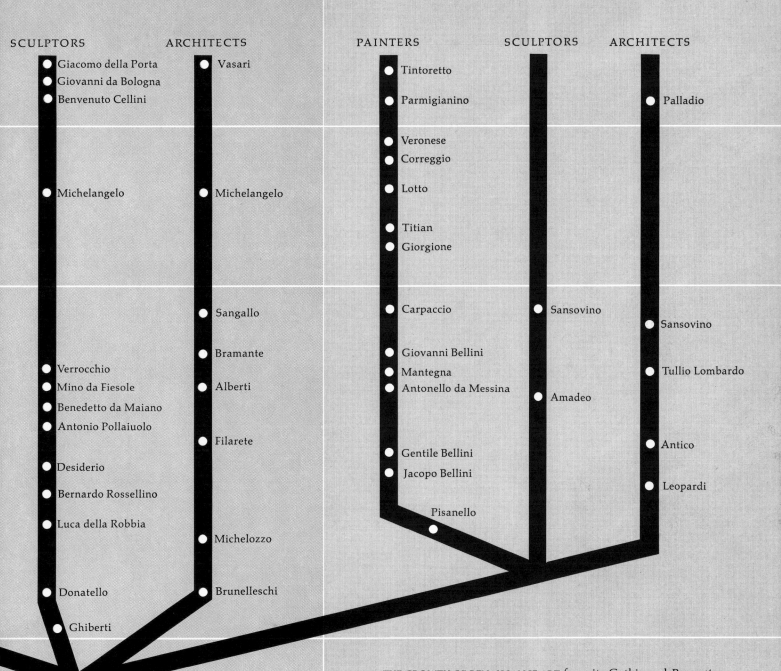

SCULPTORS

- Giacomo della Porta
- Giovanni da Bologna
- Benvenuto Cellini

- Michelangelo

- Verrocchio
- Mino da Fiesole
- Benedetto da Maiano
- Antonio Pollaiuolo

- Desiderio
- Bernardo Rossellino

- Luca della Robbia

- Donatello

- Ghiberti

- Giotto
- Cimabue

Gothic and Byzantine Art

ARCHITECTS

- Vasari

- Michelangelo

- Sangallo

- Bramante

- Alberti

- Filarete

- Michelozzo

- Brunelleschi

PAINTERS

- Tintoretto

- Parmigianino

- Veronese
- Correggio

- Lotto

- Titian
- Giorgione

- Carpaccio

- Giovanni Bellini
- Mantegna
- Antonello da Messina

- Gentile Bellini

- Jacopo Bellini

- Pisanello

SCULPTORS

- Sansovino

- Amadeo

ARCHITECTS

- Palladio

- Sansovino

- Tullio Lombardo

- Antico

- Leopardi

THE GROWTH OF RENAISSANCE ART from its Gothic and Byzantine roots is shown in this chart. The process had four phases *(far left):* the Proto-Renaissance laid the groundwork, the Renaissance formulated the style, the High Renaissance perfected it and Mannerism moved it in a new direction. Vertical divisions show the three major Italian schools. Most important was the Florentine, and the key figure in its development was Giotto. His style was further developed by Masaccio, Donatello and Brunelleschi. The artists who followed them are sometimes grouped together (e.g., the Florentine painters Andrea del Sarto and Fra Bartolommeo), indicating that they lived at the same time or that their work was related stylistically. The school of the North, dominated by Venice, represents a variation in the tradition initiated by Giotto. Siena departed least from the Proto-Renaissance tradition.

BIBLIOGRAPHY

These books were selected during the preparation of the volume for their interest and authority, and for their usefulness to readers seeking additional information on specific points. An asterisk (*) marks works available in both hard-cover and paperback editions; a dagger (†) indicates availability only in paperback.

GENERAL READING

American Heritage, *Horizon Book of the Renaissance*. Doubleday, 1961.
*Burckhardt, Jacob, *The Civilization of the Renaissance in Italy*. Transl. by S.G.C. Middlemore. London, Phaidon Press, 1960.
The Cambridge Modern History, Vol. I, *The Renaissance*. Cambridge University Press, 1907.
*Clough, Shepard B., and others, *A History of the Western World*. D. C. Heath, 1964.
Durant, Will, *The Story of Civilization*, Vol. V, *The Renaissance*. Simon & Schuster, 1953.
Ferguson, Wallace K., *Europe in Transition, 1300-1520*. Houghton Mifflin, 1962.
†Ferguson, Wallace K., and others, *Facets of the Renaissance*. Harper Torchbooks, 1963.
*Ferguson, Wallace K., and others, *The Renaissance: Six Essays*. Peter Smith, 1962.
*Gilmore, Myron P., *The World of Humanism, 1453-1517*. Harper & Row, 1952.
*Guicciardini, Francesco, *History of Italy and Other Writings*. Transl. by Cecil Grayson. Twayne Publishers, 1964.
Hay, Denys, *The Italian Renaissance in its Historical Background*. Cambridge University Press, 1962.
Jacob, E. F., ed., *Italian Renaissance Studies*. Barnes & Noble, 1960.
Lucas, Henry S., *The Renaissance and the Reformation*. Harper & Row, 1960.
The New Cambridge Modern History, Vol. I, *The Renaissance*. Cambridge University Press, 1957; Vol. II, *The Reformation*. Cambridge University Press, 1958.
†Plumb, J. H., *The Italian Renaissance*. Harper Torchbooks, 1965.
The Shorter Cambridge Medieval History. Vol. II, *The 12th Century to the Renaissance*. Cambridge University Press, 1952.
*Symonds, John Addington, *The Renaissance in Italy*. 3 vols. Peter Smith, 1961.
†Thompson, James W., and others, *The Civilization of the Renaissance*. Frederick Ungar, 1959.

POLITICS AND SOCIETY

Baron, H., *The Crisis of the Early Italian Renaissance*. 2 vols. Princeton University Press, 1955.
Brucker, Gene A., *Florentine Politics and Society, 1343-1378*. Princeton University Press, 1962.
Castiglione, Baldesar, *The Book of the Courtier*. Transl. by Charles S. Singleton. Doubleday Anchor Books, 1959.
Della Casa, Giovanni, *Galateo*. Transl. by R. S. Pine-Coffin. Penguin Books, 1958.
De Roover, Raymond, *The Rise and Decline of the Medici Bank, 1397-1494*. Harvard University Press, 1963.
Hicks, David L., "Sienese Society in the Renaissance," *Comparative Studies in Society and History*, Vol. 2, No. 4 (July 1960).
Hutton, Edward, *Florence*. David McKay, 1952.
Lucas-Dubreton, Jean, *Daily Life in Florence in the Time of the Medici*. Transl. by A. Lytton Sells. Macmillan, 1961.
*McCarthy, Mary, *The Stones of Florence*. Harcourt, Brace & World, 1959.
*McCarthy, Mary, *Venice Observed*. Reynal & Company, 1956.
*Machiavelli, Niccolò, *The Prince and the Discourses*. Modern Library, 1940.
†Martin, Alfred von, *Sociology of the Renaissance*. Harper Torchbooks, 1963.
*Mattingly, Garrett, *Renaissance Diplomacy*. Houghton Mifflin, 1955.
Schevill, Ferdinand, *Medieval and Renaissance Florence*. 2 vols. Harper Torchbooks, 1963.

THOUGHT AND CULTURE

*Cassirer, Ernst, Paul O. Kristeller and John H. Randall, Jr., eds., *Renaissance Philosophy of Man*. University of Chicago Press, 1948.
Chastel, André, *The Age of Humanism: Europe 1480-1530*. McGraw-Hill, 1963.
Ferguson, Wallace K., *The Renaissance in Historical Thought*. Houghton Mifflin, 1948.
*Kristeller, Paul O., *Renaissance Thought*. Peter Smith, 1963.
†Kristeller, Paul O., *Renaissance Thought II*. Harper Torchbooks, 1965.
Reese, Gustave, *Music in the Renaissance*. W. W. Norton & Co., 1959.
*Ross, James Bruce, and Mary Martin McLaughlin, eds., *The Portable Renaissance Reader*. Viking Press, 1953.
Sanctis, Francesco de, *History of Italian Literature*. 2 vols. Transl. by Joan Redfern. Basic Books, 1960.
Wilkins, Ernest H., *A History of Italian Literature*. Harvard University Press, 1954.
*Woodward, William H., *Vittorino da Feltre and Other Humanist Educators*. Teachers College, Columbia University, 1963.

ART AND ARCHITECTURE

*Berenson, Bernard, *Italian Painters of the Renaissance*. Phaidon Publishers, 1957.
DeWald, Ernest T., *Italian Painting, 1200-1600*. Holt, Rinehart & Winston, 1961.
Fletcher, Banister, *A History of Architecture*. Scribner, 1961.
†Holt, Elizabeth G., ed., *A Documentary History of Art*. 2 vols. Doubleday Anchor Books, 1958.
Janson, Horst W., *History of Art*. Prentice-Hall and Harry N. Abrams, 1963.
Larousse Encyclopedia of Renaissance and Baroque Art. Ed. by René Huyghe. Prometheus Press, 1964.
†Meiss, Millard, *Painting in Florence and Siena after the Black Death*. Harper Torchbooks, 1964.
Murray, Peter J., *The Architecture of the Italian Renaissance*. Schocken Books, 1964.
†Murray, Peter and Linda, *A Dictionary of Art and Artists*. Penguin Books, 1964.
*Panofsky, Erwin, *Studies in Iconology*. Peter Smith, 1962.
Pope-Hennessy, John, *Italian Renaissance Sculpture*. Phaidon Publishers, 1958.
*Vasari, Giorgio, *The Lives of the Painters, Sculptors and Architects*. 4 vols. Transl. by A. B. Hinds. Dutton, Everyman's Library, 1963.
Vermeule, Cornelius, *European Art and the Classical Past*. Harvard University Press, 1964.
Wittkower, Rudolf and Margot, *Born Under Saturn*. Random House, 1963.
*Wölfflin, Heinrich, *Art of the Italian Renaissance*. Schocken Books, 1963.

BIOGRAPHY

†Ady, Cecilia M., *Lorenzo dei Medici and Renaissance Italy*. Collier Books, 1962.
*Hale, John R., *Machiavelli and Renaissance Italy*. Macmillan, 1961.
Leonardo da Vinci. Reynal & Company, 1956.
†Plumb, J. H., ed., *Renaissance Profiles*. Harper Torchbooks, 1965.
Ridolfi, Roberto, *The Life of Niccolò Machiavelli*. Transl. by Cecil Grayson. University of Chicago Press, 1963.
†Roeder, Ralph, *The Man of the Renaissance*. Meridian Books, 1960.
†Vespasiano, *Renaissance Princes, Popes, and Prelates: Lives of Illustrious Men of the XVth Century*. Transl. by William George and Emily Waters. Harper Torchbooks, 1963.

ART INFORMATION AND PICTURE CREDITS

The sources for the illustrations in this book are set forth below. Descriptive notes on the works of art are included. Credits for pictures positioned from left to right are separated by semicolons, from top to bottom by dashes. Photographers' names which follow a descriptive note appear in parentheses. Abbreviations include "c." for century and "ca." for circa.

Cover—*Head of a Warrior*, copy of a drawing by Michelangelo (now lost), black chalk, 16th c., British Museum, London (Alinari).

CHAPTER 1: 10—Detail from the *Cantoria* by Luca della Robbia, marble bas-relief, 1431-1438, Museo del Duomo, Florence (Gjon Mili). 15—*Christ Disputing with the Doctors* by the Master of the Resurrection, majolica, 1510, Victoria and Albert Museum, London. 19—*Piero de' Medici* by Mino da Fiesole, marble portrait bust, 1453, Museo Nazionale, Florence (Alinari). 21—*Portrait of Andrea Odoni* by Lorenzo Lotto, oil on canvas, 1527, Hampton Court, Collection of Her Majesty The Queen, copyright reserved. 22-23—*The Roman Forum* by Paul Brill, oil on copper, 16th c., Doria-Pamphili Gallery, Rome (David Lees). 24—*Boy Reading Cicero* by Vincenzo Foppa, fresco, ca. 1460, The Wallace Collection, London (Derek Bayes). 25—*St. Jerome in his Study*, presumed portrait of Cardinal Bessarion, by Vittore Carpaccio, oil painting, 1502-1507, Scuola di San Giorgio degli Schiavoni, Venice (Marzari). 26—*The Three Graces*, Pompeian wall painting, fresco, 1st c. A.D., Museo Nazionale, Naples (Scala); *The Three Graces*, Italian manuscript illumination, 14th c., The British Museum, London. 27—Detail from *Primavera* by Botticelli, oil painting, ca. 1478, Galleria degli Uffizi, Florence (Marzari). 28-29—*The School of Athens* by Raphael, fresco, 1509-1511, Stanza della Segnatura, Vatican, Rome (David Lees).

CHAPTER 2: 30—The Baptistery at Pisa (Roloff Beny). 33—*Pope and Emperor*, print, ca., 1470, Gabinetto dei Disegni, Galleria degli Uffizi, Florence (Walter Sanders). 34—*Payday at the Venetian Arsenal*, engraving, early 17th c., New York Public Library (Frank H. Bauer). 36—*Bocche di leone*, stone, 16th c., Ducal Palace, Venice (Roloff Beny). 39—Detail from *The Departure of St. Ursula* by Vittore Carpaccio, oil painting, 1490-1496, Gallerie dell'Accademia, Venice (Emmett Bright). 40—Gondolas at the edge of the Grand Canal in Venice (Bernard G. Silberstein from Rapho-Guillumette). 41—Detail from *The Healing of the Demoniac* by Vittore Carpaccio, oil painting, 1494, Gallerie dell'Accademia, Venice (Emmett Bright). 42—Pine forest near Classe (James Burke)—detail from *Procession of the Magi* by Benozzo Gozzoli, fresco, 1459, Medici-Riccardi Palace, Florence (Marzari). 43—*The Fruit Vendor* by Vincenzo Campi, oil painting, 2nd half 16th c., Pinacoteca di Brera, Milan (Scala)—*Young Girls Bathing* by Bernardino Luini, fresco, 1520-1525, Pinacoteca di Brera, Milan (Marzari). 44—View of Florence (David Lees)—detail of *Charles V Besieging Florence* by Giorgio Vasari, fresco, 1530, Palazzo Vecchio, Florence (Erich Lessing from Magnum). 45—*Sheltering Pilgrims* by Francisco Hubertini Bacchiacca, oil painting on wood panel, ca. 1550, Rijksmuseum, Amsterdam. 46—Villa near Spoleto (Dori Watson). 46-47—Detail from *The Assassination of St. Peter Martyr* attributed to Giovanni Bellini, oil painting, ca. 1500, The National Gallery, London (Derek Bayes). 48—Casale Marco Simone, northeast of Rome (Aldo Durazzi)—*Giving Lodging to the Pilgrim* from the School of Ghirlandaio, fresco, 2nd half of 15th c., San Martino dei Buonomini (Scala). 49—*Feeding the Hungry* by Santi Viviani, majolica frieze, 1526-1528, Ospedale del Ceppo, Pistoia (David Lees). 50—*Pilgrim Group* by Santi Viviani, majolica frieze, Ospedale del Ceppo, Pistoia (David Lees). 51—*The Seven Churches of Rome* by Antoine Lafrery, engraving, 1575, original in black and white, Gabinetto delle Stampe, Rome (Oscar Savio).

CHAPTER 3: 52—Detail of *Christ and St. Thomas* by Andrea del Verrocchio, bronze, 1478-1483, Tabernacolo di Mercanzia, Orsanmichele, Florence (David Lees). 55—Page from *Aritmetica* by Filippo Calandri, woodcut, 1491, The Metropolitan Museum of Art, New York, Rodgers Fund, 1919. 59—*Studies of Costume* by Antonio Pisanello, pen-and-ink

ACKNOWLEDGMENTS

The editors are indebted to David L. Hicks, Associate Professor of History, New York University; Bruno Molajoli, Director of Fine Arts and Antiquities for Italy, Ministry of Public Instruction, Rome; Ugo Procacci, Superintendent of Galleries, Florence; Luciano Berti, Director of National Museum, Florence; Luisa Beccherucci, Directress of Uffizi Galleries, Florence; Irma Merolle-Tondi, Directress of Laurentian Library, Florence; Piero Aranguren, Director of Historical Museum, Florence; Sergio Camerani, Director of State Archives, Florence; Mario Ristori, State Archives, Florence; Rodolfo Francioni, Director of l'Opera del Duomo, Florence; Rolf Rapp-Nives Poli, Complesso Fiorentino di Musica Antica, Florence; Silio Sensi, Superintendency of Galleries, Florence; Mario Bernocchi, Prato; Alessandro Prosdicini, Director, Civic Museum, Padua; Eugenio Premuda and Giuseppe Ungaro, Institute of the History of Medicine, Padua University; Deoclecio Redig de Campos, Vatican Museum, Vatican City; Ugo Bianchi, Photographic Archive, Vatican Museum, Vatican City; Giovanni Antonelli, State Archives, Viminal Palace, Rome; Italo Faldi, Director, Palazzo Doria Gallery, Rome; Angelo Monteverdi, President, Accademia dei Lincei, Rome; General Arnaldo Forgiero and Colonel Eugenio Panasci, Castel Sant' Angelo, Rome; Francesco Valcanover, Director of the Academy Gallery, Venice; Giovanni Mariacher, Director of Correr Museum, Venice; Giuseppe Marchini, Superintendent of the Galleries of the Marches, Urbino; Filippa Maria Aliberti, Superintendress of the Galleries of the Marches, Urbino; Academy of Fine Arts, Ravenna; Savino Melone, Director, National Museum of Science and Technology, Milan; Luigi Crema, Superintendent of Monuments for Lombardy, Milan; Giovanni Paccagnini, Superintendent of Galleries, Mantua; Gilberto Carra, Archivio di Stato, Mantua; Raffaello Causa, Director, Capodimonte Museum, Naples; Galleria Luigi Bellini, Florence; National Gallery, London; and Department of Western Art, Ashmolean Museum, Oxford.

INDEX

This symbol in front of a page number indicates a photograph or painting of the subject mentioned.